I0665059

PIRATE MOON
& OTHER STORIES

DAVID HEALEY

INTRACOASTAL

PIRATE MOON & Other Stories (Collected Fiction and Essays)

By David Healey

Copyright © 2019 by David Healey. All rights reserved. No part of this book may be used or reproduced by any means without the written permission of the publisher except in the case of brief quotation for the purpose of critical articles and reviews. Please support the arts by refusing to pirate creative content.

Intracoastal Media digital edition published 2019. Print edition published 2019. ISBN 978-0-9674162-1-2

This book is a work of fiction and creative nonfiction. Names, characters, places and incidents are products of the author's imagination or are used fictitiously. Any resemblance to actual events or locales or persons, living or dead, is entirely coincidental.

BISAC Subject Headings:

LCO002000 LITERARY COLLECTIONS / American / General

FIC029000 FICTION / Short Stories (single author)

In memory of Donald C. Herring
Editor, mentor, and teacher

The night came softly down, as nowhere else except upon the skies of the Delaware and Chesapeake.

— GEORGE ALFRED TOWNSEND, TALES OF THE CHESAPEAKE, 1880

CONTENTS

Preface   ix

Enchanter   1
Trivial Pursuit   11
The House That Brewed Up Trouble   17
Legal Issues   40
Seeker   54
Cream Soda   69
Road Trip   70
Pirate Moon   73
The Midnight Service   82
The Fox Went Out On A Chilly Night   88
Last Stand at Turkey Point Light   91
Bullet Baby   105
The Wheatfield War   112
Cole's Sojourn   120
Gray Ghosts   140
Novel Run: Reflections on Writing and Running   161
Writer's Choice: William Styron, White Wine, and   163
the Power of Imagination
The Accidental Librarian   166
Snapshot: The Day Nixon Resigned—August 9, 1974   169
Born In A Greenhouse   171
Trapline   174
Memorial Day: Medals & Memories of World War II   178
Vacation Dreaming   183
Heirloom Tomatoes   186
Life's Rich Compost   189
Delmarvese   192
Glass Beach   195

About the Author   199

PREFACE

We are all storytellers in some way, aren't we? Some of us just happen to write them down as we go along. Compiling this book has made me realize how lucky I am to have grown up in a family that liked to tell stories and to have been around a lot of natural storytellers.

My father still spins a good story and my mother was a keen observer who also came from a long line of storytellers. Sometimes, I don't know whether to blame them or thank them for passing that along. Some more practical skills in, say, mechanical engineering, might have led to a more lucrative career. Mostly, though, I think I'd thank them for sharing that love for a good story.

The great writing coach James N. Frey has said that kids who grow up to be writers are usually the ones who had their imagination prodded in some way. He gives the example of a kid who comes across a banana peel on the ground and asks where it came from. An adult from a no-nonsense kind of family would respond that someone dropped it there, obviously. End of story. But in a storytelling family, one of the adults will point up at the trees and say, "The monkey who lives in that tree must have dropped it."

Naturally, the next question is, "What monkey?"

And thus begins a spontaneous story of one kind or another. Frey says those kids who are invited to imagine are the ones who grow up to write novels because they're always trying to tell the story of the monkey in the tree.

You won't find a monkey in any of these stories, although there are pirates, German commandos, killer lawyers, and even a wily fox. Along with that monkey business, I've also been fortunate to live my life in an area rich with stories—if you know where to look for them and if you are willing to listen.

I can still remember some of the old-timers telling me about how their grandparents hid the horses in the woods when the Union troops marched by. For them, the Civil War was still within living memory. It was something that had touched the lives of their families in very real ways. Again and again, if you're willing to listen, you will hear stories like that across the region. I also have a theory that old places and old houses soak up history and radiate it back in the same way that a stone wall gives off warmth at night after absorbing sunshine all day. You just have to be willing to open your senses and feel it.

These stories and essays go back nearly forty years, to a short story called "The Fox Went Out On A Chilly Night," published in a local magazine. Back then I was in my full-blown teenage Hemingway mode, working my way through everything—and I mean everything—that the author had ever written. That is definitely the oldest story here and I have tried not to change a word of what my sixteen-year-old self wrote. The most recent story is "The House That Brewed Up Trouble," completed just a few weeks before publication. Some stories, like "Bullet Baby," are based on actual events or legends.

Most of the published stories and essays have appeared in regional publications across Maryland and Delaware, which I now realize places me firmly in the category of being a regional writer. Sadly, some of these print publications have fallen by the wayside over the years, notably the wonderful *Delmarva Quarterly* in which I was lucky to have several essays published.

It's a strange journey, going back and revisiting these old stories and essays. It's a bit like looking at old pictures of yourself and wondering why you ever thought that wearing terrycloth wristbands and those tube socks that went up to your knees was a good idea. Revising these stories has also been a lot like time traveling. Almost all of the stories and a few of the essays have been revised in some way, sometimes substantially. The notes at the ends of the pieces recognize that fact. Just to be clear on the difference, a "story" by my definition is pure fiction while an "essay" is more of a commentary or observation on some slice of life, from meeting author William Styron to growing tomatoes to running a trapline. For the purposes of this book, I have tried to include only those essays with some regional focus. There is no narrative order here ... feel free to dip in at random and skip around.

These stories and essays have been enjoyable to write over the years and then to revisit here. Most of them have been a labor of love in that unlike most of my newspaper articles or even some of my books, they weren't written on deadline or for a paycheck. I sincerely hope that you enjoy reading them—just keep an eye out for that monkey in the tree!

Finally, I want to thank the many individuals who have been so supportive in my own journey as a writer. This includes many colleagues and co-workers over the years, as well as understanding family and friends. A special thanks goes to my father for his starring role in two of the essays. I also want to thank the editors of the publications named here. I would be remiss not to express appreciation to the region's many wonderful bookstores for their amazing support of local authors.

It's hard to single out any one person, but you will notice that the book is dedicated to Don Herring, longtime editor of the *Cecil Whig* newspaper. Don was a gifted writer and a natural teacher who helped dozens of young reporters understand the importance of accuracy as well as the beauty in a clear and concise sentence.

Beyond the daily paper, one project that Don and I worked on together was *A History of the Cecil Whig*, published back in 1992 for the 150th anniversary of the newspaper. Don was the author and my role was to serve as a researcher and copyeditor, which meant that for me, each day became a writing lesson from one of the best.

Again, thank you for reading and please be sure to stay in touch at www.davidhealeyauthor.com

DH
Chesapeake City, Maryland
2019

STORIES

Turkey Point Lighthouse, Chesapeake Bay

ENCHANTER

Nobody saw *Enchanter* arrive. She came during the night, quiet as a dream, and tied up at the town dock.

That summer, I was working for the town, doing everything from cutting grass to painting the band shell and park benches. The yacht was there when I drove down to the waterfront early one morning to empty the trash cans.

"Is it all right if we tie up here?" a man on the bow called out to me. He was tall and lean, with an air about him that smelled of money. Living in a tourist town, you get so you can smell the money on people.

"You can tie up overnight," I said, lifting a trash can out of its concrete holder. "There's a twenty-four hour limit."

"Well, there might be a bit of a problem with that," he said. "You see, we've broken down. We'd need a tugboat to budge her."

I looked the yacht over, wondering who the "we" might be. *Enchanter* was a beautiful yacht, a good fifty feet long, her tall structure and sleek white fiberglass making her look like some oversized swan that was huddled alongside the town pier.

"It's only Monday morning, so I don't suppose anyone would

mind," I said. "On the weekends, all the local boaters want to tie up at the pier because, it's free."

"Well, thank you," the man said, as if I had just done him a big favor. He came up close to the pier and reached a long arm across to offer his hand. I had to put down the trash can to shake it. He had a firm grip and friendly eyes. "I'm Louis Beauford."

"Jimmy Duncan," I said. Instantly, I liked this man. As I found out later—as we all found out—he was good at making people like him.

"What town is this?" called a woman's voice.

I looked up. A woman had emerged onto the deck. She wore sporty yachting clothes, white slacks and a navy blue pullover and gold jewelry.

"This is my wife," Beauford announced. "Amanda, this is Jimmy Duncan."

Mrs. Beauford looked right at me. She had the bluest eyes I had ever seen—they leapt out of the tan face. She was much younger than her husband, blond, and looked something like Michelle Pfeiffer, the actress.

"Well?" she asked, and I realized that I'd been staring at her longer than was polite and still hadn't answered her question.

"Chesapeake City," I managed, having temporarily forgotten where I lived. Then, not knowing what else to do, I dumped the trash out into the back of the pickup.

When I look up again, Amanda Beauford was still watching me. Before she turned and went below, she gave me this little smile that lasted me the rest of the day.

By NOON, the whole town knew about *Enchanter*, and it seemed everyone had met "Louis and Amanda." They weren't like the rich boaters who usually stopped in town. Louis introduced himself to everyone like a politician or a bank president would, and seemed really interested in the people he met as if even old

Mrs. Smith had the most interesting stories to tell about her cat and her bursitis.

Amanda looked like a model, so every man in town was glad to talk to her. The women in town might have been jealous of the attention she received, but Amanda was so friendly and genuine that even the wives and girlfriends liked her. Besides, they had Louis to flirt with, and he seemed glad to oblige.

The Beaufords had lunch in the café. They sat at the counter and chatted with whoever came in—mostly locals, since it was Monday.

"Jimmy," Mr. Beauford said, remembering my name from that morning. "I understand you work part-time for the town."

"It's just a summer job," explained. I didn't add that for a 16-year-old it was a great job, getting to drive the town truck and everyone treating me like an adult for a change.

"Maybe you'd have time to do a little work for us," Mr. Beauford said, smiling hopefully. "Our *Enchanter* could use a good scrubbing down. We just came up Chesapeake Bay, and the bow is brown from all the mud and algae in the water. Interested?"

"Sure," I said with a shrug. Mrs. Beauford was looking at me over the rim of her glass of ice tea as she took a sip and I felt myself blushing.

"Good man," he said. "Stop by the boat after you finish up your town job for the day and I'll show you what to do."

When Mr. and Mrs. Beauford finished lunch, he patted down his pockets, then announced, obviously alarmed, that he must have left his wallet on the boat. "Stay here, darling," he said to his wife. "I'll just run and get some money."

From the other side of the counter, Betty called out and stopped him before he could run out the door. "You can catch up with me later," she said, then laughed. "I know you're good for it."

With an embarrassed smile, Mr. Beauford thanked her and the couple walked out.

"Ain't that something," said Bobby Tull, who worked at

Canal Marina. "Rich people like that and they don't even have any money on them."

"Oh, they've got plenty of money, honey," Betty said. "All you've got to do is take a look at their boat to know that. I'll bet they could buy this whole town if they wanted."

Everybody laughed because it was probably true.

Before the weekend came, Louis—nobody thought to call him "Louie" or "Lou"—was friends with just about everybody in town. He was always in one shop or another talking to folks or having lunch at the café. One thing for sure was that Mr. Beauford was different from just about any other tourist who had ever come to town.

Maybe it was because he had time on his hands while *Enchanter* was being fixed, but it only took a few days for him to become a fixture in town as much as any of us locals.

One way or another, just about everyone in Chesapeake City made their living from the tourists who flooded our town every summer. Most of us who had grown up here or lived in town for years took the scenery for granted, but it took people like the Beaufords to help us see it with fresh eyes.

There are a lot of old houses in town and a lot of history from when the town was a port of call on the Chesapeake and Delaware Canal, with its own lock. Visitors came to soak all that in, or else they came to sit on a bench and eat ice cream along the waterfront. *Enchanter* became something of a tourist attraction in itself that summer, with folks daydreaming about how nice it must be to own a yacht.

MOSTLY, Mrs. Beauford stayed on the yacht. She was either inside, out of sight behind the tinted windows, or up on the top deck, where the gawkers couldn't see her.

"You're doing a good job, Jimmy," she called down over the

rail. I was in a rowboat alongside *Enchanter*, scrubbing the brown stains off her bow with a long-handled brush.

"Where has this boat been, Mrs. Beauford?" I called up. "There's so much gunk on here it looks like you've been traveling forever."

"You missed a spot," she said, pointing. I noticed that she didn't answer my question. "When you're finished, bring that brush up here, please. The seagulls have been making a mess."

It was another hour before I rowed the boat in and carried the bucket and brush up to the top deck. Mrs. Beauford was in a one-piece swimsuit, stretched out on a chaise lounge, reading a magazine and looking more like Michelle Pfeiffer than ever. She looked up, but I couldn't see those blue eyes because of her sunglasses.

"See what I mean about the seagulls?" she said.

The deck did need a good scrubbing, but it wasn't just the birds to blame. More like grime in general. From a distance, even from the pier, *Enchanter* appeared to be gleaming and spotless. But when you got up close, she had a veneer of dust and dirt that never quite seemed to scrub off.

I dipped the brush in the bucket and went to work. I could feel Mrs. Beauford watching me.

By the time I was finished, the magazine was across her chest and I thought she was asleep, although I couldn't be sure on account of the sunglasses.

BEFORE ANYONE KNEW IT, *Enchanter* had been tied up at the town pier for most of July. This was against the rules, of course, because only overnight docking was allowed. However, it wasn't the first time that a boat had stayed longer than a week or two—it was just that the *Enchanter* was the biggest boat to do it. Nobody really enforced the rule, anyhow, and Louis Beauford was practically best friends with the mayor by then.

The yacht needed a lot of work. Joey Wilson went aboard to do some plumbing work, and Ed Wilkes spent a few days going over the electronics aboard. There were some problems with the engine, too, and Bobby Tull came over from Canal Marina to work on those. Mr. Beauford didn't have a car, so the mayor let him borrow his station wagon to drive the six miles into Elkton to do some banking and other errands. Another day he and Mrs. Beauford drove all the way to Christiana Mall to do some shopping for things you just couldn't get in Chesapeake City.

Lunchtimes at the café, Bobby Tull was always in a good mood. "That yacht of the Beaufords' needs a lot of work. I mean, a lot. By the time I get done, I'll be able to buy me a new pickup truck."

"You should see the fuel bill for that yacht," said Mike Everett, who had delivered the diesel in a tanker truck because the yacht couldn't move from the dock. "I could pay my mortgage for a couple of months for what it cost to fill those tanks. They were damn near empty."

"And you should see the Beaufords' tab here," Betty put in. "Louis comes in for breakfast and lunch, and sometimes Amanda comes with him."

"And every night they eat at one of the restaurants in town," Billy said. "The Bohemia House is one of their favorites."

Someone gave a low whistle, and we knew what he meant. Entrees started at twenty-five dollars at the restaurant.

"Must be nice to be rich," Betty said, and sighed.

EVERYONE WAS IMPRESSED when Mr. Beauford invited the whole town to a birthday party for his wife and announced the party would be catered by the Bohemia House. It was getting near the end of July; the summer season was in full swing. He set the party for a Thursday night so everyone who had to make a living with the tourists on the weekends could come.

Mr. and Mrs. Beauford both dressed all in white and they made quite a couple—just like they had stepped out of some magazine or maybe even out of a movie. The party was in Pell Gardens, the town park down by the waterfront, and I set up speakers in the windows of *Enchanter*, so that there was music for the evening. It was a great party, just like a big, fancy wedding reception.

I stayed after most of the parents and little kids went home. The party was still going strong, and I was sitting on a bench with Bobby Tull's daughter, Jennifer. Just beyond *Enchanter* we could see the open canal, lined with the yellow-orange navigation lights stretching into the distance. A pleasure boat—much smaller than *Enchanter*—was heading east toward the Delaware Bay.

"Hello, Jimmy." I felt a hand on my shoulder and looked up to see Mrs. Beauford standing there. "Who's your friend?"

"This is Jennifer, Mrs. Beauford."

She squeezed my shoulder, sending what felt like an electric current right down through the soles of my sneakers. I could smell the alcohol on her breath. "Jimmy, darling Jimmy. Just sixteen years old."

Jennifer touched my arm. "Come on, Jimmy."

As Jennifer steered me away, I asked, "What's the hurry?"

"I don't like her," Jennifer whispered.

Mrs. Beauford called out, "Good luck to you, darling Jimmy."

As Mrs. Beauford walked unsteadily away, Jennifer said, "She's drunk. And why is she telling you good luck? Is she going away?"

"I don't think so," I said.

We stayed out late, hanging with the other teens on the playground equipment behind the elementary school, sneaking cigarettes and slapping at mosquitos. If we'd thought about it, we'd have realized that it was pretty much what our parents had done on this same playground twenty-five years ago. From time to time, couples sneaked away into the dark, me and Jennifer included. It was close to midnight when I walked Jennifer home and went to bed.

Sometime during the night, *Enchanter* slipped away.

IN THE MORNING, it was strange to see the dock empty. Everyone in town was mystified about the Beaufords disappearing like that, even though folks agreed it was a wonderful party, and very nice of the Beaufords to invite everyone.

The only thing left behind was a package on the dock addressed to, "Our friends in Chesapeake City." Nobody was quite sure who should open it, so we left it sitting on the bench where it had been left.

Without the Beaufords or their yacht, the town felt as dull and hollow as the morning after Christmas. The couple had brought a touch of glamor and excitement to town that had kind of crept over us and we only noticed now that they were gone.

At three o'clock, a sheriff's deputy drove up to the town dock. I was down there hosing off the new promenade, which as a town employee was part of my job, even though I was really just hoping to get some news about when the *Enchanter* was going to return.

"Where's the yacht that was here?" the deputy asked.

"Gone," I said.

The deputy's appearance was drawing a small crowd. "Did they say where they were going?"

"No, sir."

He picked up the package addressed to "Our Friends in Chesapeake City." "I'll need to keep this as evidence," he said, then put the package in his patrol car and drove away.

I think that by then we all knew what had happened, even though we didn't want to admit it.

It still took a few days for the truth to hit home—and by then, *Enchanter* was long-gone.

Betty was the first to mention the bills they had left behind. The Beaufords had run up a $600 tab at the café.

"I should have known better," she said. "But I thought the proof that they were good for it was tied up down at the town dock."

"Well, that proof sailed away three days ago," Bobby Tull said bitterly. "They stuck me for ten grand in engine repairs."

The marine electronics weren't paid for, either, as it turned out. All over town, the shop owners reported small things they had handed over to Mr. Beauford or Mrs. Beauford when one or the other didn't have cash on them: T- shirts, books, antiques, even a painting. Like Betty at the café, everyone figured the collateral was tied up at the clock.

It turned out, too, that the Beaufords—or whoever they were, because it was becoming clear that those were not their real names—had used fake credit cards to pay for the restaurants and their shopping trip to Christiana Mall.

I never even got my money for scrubbing down the yacht.

My payment for all those hours of work came down to a cold soda Mrs. Beauford gave me.

———

A COUPLE of months went by before the package the deputy had seized was returned to town. Everyone had pretty much forgotten about it until the mayor brought it down to the café to open up after getting it back from the local state's attorney.

"You open it, Betty," the mayor said. "I don't know what in the world it could be."

"I'm not sure I want to open it after how those people hood-winked us," she said, a note of bitterness in her voice.

"Aw, go ahead."

Betty took one of her kitchen knives and sliced the packing tape. Some pages from the local paper had been balled up to protect whatever was inside. She dug around through the paper and finally pulled out a black, metal sign.

It was about two feet long and oval-shaped. On one side, in white lettering, the sign read: *Welcome to Chesapeake City*. On the other side, the one that folks would see leaving the town, was a standing invitation: *Come again*.

"Of all the nerve!" Betty cried, and slammed the sign down in disgust.

Like Betty, most people thought that the sign was the ultimate insult to injury, that it might as well have said, *Easy pickings here* or *Welcome to Suckersville*.

Then we found out the sign was the one thing the Beaufords had actually paid for—in cash—in a rush-order job at a shop in Elkton. I was working for the town again that summer now that I was in college, and the mayor told me to put it up at the entrance to town. That sign is still there today.

Enchanter never has returned. Every now and then a yacht that looks like her will appear at the town dock, and in spite of ourselves, in spite of how the Beaufords made fools of us, there's a twinge of excitement. No one will admit it out loud, but we hope it might be the *Enchanter* once again, come to bring a little magic to town.

ADAPTED from the story originally published in the *Cecil Whig* newspaper, September 10, 1999.

TRIVIAL PURSUIT

A sk me anything and I know the answer. Who made the first trans-Atlantic radio broadcast? Guglielmo Marconi in 1902. How many legs does a spider have? Eight. What color Life-saver do you find no matter which end of the roll you open first? Yellow.

Those are easy. All part of a night's work for a radio talk show host. That's what I do from midnight till 6 a.m. I chat. Just spin conversations with callers about politics, books, and the latest White House scandal. And every caller gets a chance to ask a trivia question that stumps me.

George is one of the regulars who try to get me nearly every night. He calls right about when the bars are letting out in Elsmere.

"I've been thinking about the Monica Lewinsky situation, Tom. There's something fishy about the whole thing," he says in his nasal Delmarva twang. *Feeshy*. George is a staunch conspiracy theorist.

"Go ahead and ask me a question, George," I say, hoping we can skip his latest speculation tonight.

"OK." He pauses, and I imagine his smile, thinking he's got me this time. "What is the world's smallest independent state?"

"Vatican City."

George laughs. "I can't get anything by you, Tom," he says. "If I was a pitcher and you was a batter, you'd be the guy I'd walk."

It's my turn to laugh. And then to question.

"Who was the only U.S. president with more than three syllables in his last name?"

"Aw, geez, I know this one, Tom. Hold on a minute."

"Tick, tick, tick," I say.

"James Madison—no, that's three. McKinley? No. I know it's not Roosevelt."

"Time's up, George. If you said Eisenhower you'd be right."

"OK, Tom. I'll get you next time."

I put in a slip to have a T-shirt sent to George, anyhow. He deserves one for being a regular.

"Can anybody out there answer me this?" I say into the microphone. "What 1941 movie broke the record for the longest screen kiss? Answer the question correctly and I'll send you a T-shirt."

The line lights up and a woman's voice come on.

"*You're in the Army Now*," she says. "Regis Toomey and Jane Wyman kissed for one hundred and eighty-five seconds."

"Congratulations." Someone is listening, after all. "You've just won yourself a T-shirt. Who's calling, please?"

"I'll tell you my name if you can answer this question." She has an intelligent voice, a bit breathy, like Jane Wyman sounded after that kiss. It's late, and I guess she's either a nurse just coming off her shift or else someone who can't sleep. Yet another insomniac calling.

"OK." I shrug, even though she can't see, of course. "What's the question?"

"How did the Minnesota Twins get their name?"

"They're named after the Twin Cities, Minneapolis and St. Paul."

"Mmmm," she murmurs sleepily. "I'm Marilyn."

"Well, Marilyn, what's on your mind tonight?"

"Absolutely nothing. Ask me another question."

"OK ... what actor who served as an officer in the Army Air Corps during World War II had a price put on his head by the Germans?"

"Clark Gable," she says. "My turn. How many home runs did Babe Ruth hit?"

"Seven hundred and fourteen."

She fires another question at me. It's like playing ping-pong.

"What hockey player has scored more goals than any other player in the history of the sport?"

"Wayne Gretzsky. Hah! OK, tell me this, Marilyn: What was the name of the beatnik character on the TV series, *The Dobie Gillis Show*?"

"Maynard G. Krebs. Played by Bob Denver of *Gilligan's Island* fame," Marilyn says. "How about another TV question? On *My Three Sons*, what star from another show played a character named Gilbert Thornberry?"

Good grief. How am I supposed to know that?

"I'm waiting," she says. "Tick, tick, tick."

"I give up."

"Tony Dow. You remember him, don't you, Tom? He played Wally on *Leave it to Beaver*."

She rubs it in a bit, but I can't let my annoyance be broadcast over the air. I'm also curious, intrigued by this mysterious trivia master. I say in my radio voice: "Congratulations, Marilyn. You got me. I guess you've won yourself another T-shirt. Stay on the line, please, and I'll get your address."

I switch off the mic and play a commercial so we can talk off the air.

"I don't want a T-shirt," she says.

"Well, you won it."

"Send it to somebody else, if you want. I just called because I felt like it, not to win something."

"You sound tired," I say. "Just get off work?"

"Questions, questions. You never stop, do you, Tom?"

One rule of mine is that I never get involved with callers beyond the business at hand. I don't want to know their troubles, whether or not their wife just left them, or how much they've had to drink that night. But Marilyn has a nice voice although voices can be deceiving and she sounds, well, flirtatious. And so I ask. Pure impulse.

"I know this is kind of crazy. But are you doing anything for lunch tomorrow?" Even as I say it I know how foolish I'm being. She's probably married! Or she has a live-in boyfriend who's six-four. My palms start sweating.

"That's another question," Marilyn says.

"Sorry. Well?"

"If you want a date, you have to win it from me."

"Huh?"

"I won a shirt from you, right? You have to win a date. I'll call back tomorrow night." And then she's gone.

Our trouble is that we've become a nation of trivia lovers. We're proud of our grasp of disconnected facts. Look at games we play or watch on TV: Trivial Pursuit, *Jeopardy*. All those ridiculous game shows.

Some people believe facts pass for knowledge, but knowledge is like a deep well, while trivia is merely a shallow puddle left by a lifelong rain of television, movies and newspapers. Who cares if Tony Dow made a guest appearance on *Father Knows Best*? In the scheme of things, it doesn't matter.

Who cares, either, about a date with some woman named Marilyn? But in the morning her voice echoes in my ear. Sounding tired, sleepy. Questioning.

Later on I find myself flipping through my *World Almanac*. Then I walk down the street to buy a stack of newspapers. Cramming on account of Marilyn.

That night, I've settled in for the early morning hours when she calls. Most of Wilmington is sleeping. When I look out the studio window I can see that even I-95 is nearly empty. Somewhere out there my wakeful listeners are holed up with their radios and cigarettes, their coffee or booze.

A line lights up. "Hello, Tom," she says.

"There's my trivia master." I'd rather tell her I'm glad she called or ask if she still wanted to go through with this, but we're on the air.

"I've got a question for you tonight, Tom."

"Just one?" I have dozens for her, scratched down on a legal pad beside the mic.

"Only one question," she says. "If you answer it, you win our little wager."

Listeners must be wondering what we've bet. They'll be leaning closer to their radios.

"OK. Go ahead."

Marilyn pauses for effect. "What is the first sentence in *A Tale of Two Cities* by Charles Dickens?"

You might know that sentence, and you might be reading this, feeling smug, or mentally shouting the answer at me. Isn't that part of the fun of trivia? You get to test yourself, and if you know the answer and you're listening to the contestant mumbling to himself, all you can do is yell at the radio. Well, shout a little louder, will you?

I hope you'll get through to me, because I can't remember. It's a common trivia question, so common that people who didn't even read the novel in high school know the opening line. I've read the book and all I draw is a blank.

"Tick, tick, tick." Marilyn's voice in my ear.

"Give me a minute. I know this."

Do I? Ah, the pointlessness of trivia. Our minds in their accumulation of useless facts become like the junk drawer in the kitchen that holds rubber bands, twist ties, scissors, bits of string, expired coupons, and a recipe of chili. It's hard to believe we're proud of being able to dig through this jumble in our brains, like we might dig out a candle and a book of matches when the lights go out.

" 'It was the best of times, it was the worst of times,' " I finally answer. I kill the mic, run a commercial.

"Took you long enough," she says playfully.

"But I got it right."

"You win, then."

"How does Caprio's sound? Say at noon tomorrow?"

"More questions." Marilyn laughs. It's a sound that makes me smile. "The answer is that I'll see you there. Just look for the dirty blond in a dark blue sweater. I'm outrageously gorgeous. What do you look like?"

"Clark Gable."

I can almost hear her smile over the line. "Tomorrow, then, Mr. Gable."

There are a few hours to go before the morning news crew shows up, and George has yet to call with his latest conspiracy theory. I'm still flying after winning lunch with Marilyn, and I can't focus enough to fill the airwaves with chatter. So I stop, take a sip of coffee, and to buy myself some time, ask, "Now, for a T-shirt, can anyone out there name the town where Lawrence Welk was born?"

ORIGINALLY PUBLISHED IN *Out & About* magazine, September 1998.

THE HOUSE THAT BREWED UP
TROUBLE

E ven before Maggie Delpino was mugged on the snowy street out front, that evening's gathering was well on its way to going down in the annals of the Chesapeake City Book Club as being particularly memorable. The evening had been a perfect trifecta of great coffee and desserts at the Café on the Bay, a good book to discuss, and an interesting show and tell by Maggie, who had brought along a signed poster from the movie that had been made from that night's book, *The Blue Max* by Jack D. Hunter.

Never mind that the book had been a bestseller more than fifty years before and then made into a movie in 1966 with some of the biggest stars of the day. The book still resonated because the author had lived in Chesapeake City and invested some of his literary windfall in fixing up old houses in town. Decades later, *The Blue Max* kept us turning pages.

"Loved it!" said Maggie, who was among the first to get ready to leave. The movie poster was in a protective cardboard tube tucked under her arm. "I'm going to get going because I've got this tickle in my throat from a cold coming on and I want to get home before this snow gets any worse."

I checked my phone. "The forecast says we're getting a foot of snow."

Maggie groaned. "I guess there's no point in even opening my shop tomorrow. Between the rain all summer and now the snow, how am I supposed to stay in business!"

On her way out the door, however, Maggie got to chatting and it was Leslie Hammond who actually left first, throwing on her coat and disappearing into the growing storm with barely a goodbye. Then Maggie followed a few minutes later.

No one heard Maggie scream, because at that moment Tammy had turned on the machine to whip the cream for a final hot cocoa that Mac ordered. Another ten minutes went by before anyone left the café and found Maggie in the snow, bleeding from a blow to the head and struggling to get her feet under her on the icy street.

That's when all the warmth and charm went out of the evening, as if whisked away by the cold wind of the nor'easter coming down the Chesapeake and Delaware Canal.

I was the first one to reach Maggie's side and I tried to help her up, but we were both having some trouble getting our footing. Mac appeared at her other side, towering over us both and looking more like the Abominable Snowman as snow began to coat his shoulders and hair.

"You must have slipped," I said, holding Maggie steady. "Are you OK?"

Maggie touched her scalp, her fingers coming away bloody. She must have hit the pavement hard. "My head hurts," she said, clearly in pain. "And I think that I banged my knee."

"Let's get you inside and have a look," I said. "It's too cold out here."

Other members of the book club had come out and Maggie was at the center of a huddle of concern as everyone moved back into the warmth of the café. I was glad that Maggie wasn't hurt worse because due to the deepening snow, I wasn't sure that it would be easy for an ambulance to get to the hospital a few miles away in the county seat.

Back inside, I said, "I'm glad that you didn't break anything when you fell."

"I didn't fall," Maggie said. "I was pushed. Hit in the head first, and then pushed."

A hush fell over the huddle. Muggings did not happen in Chesapeake City. Besides, what could Maggie possibly have had of any value?

"Are you sure?"

She glared at me, angry now. "He took my poster! Ripped it right out of my hands! And then he shoved me hard and ran off."

"Did you get a look at him?"

Maggie shook her head, still clearly stunned. "He was wearing a mask or maybe a scarf. I couldn't see his face."

I looked at Mac, who was my business partner and longtime friend. At six-foot-four with a build like a refrigerator, Mac also happened to be an ex-cop. He was a good guy to have watching your back when a mugger was on the loose. "Let's go see if we can find anything out there," I said.

With the exception of me, Mac, and the café owner's boyfriend, the book club was made up of women. They clucked with concern over Maggie, getting her ice for the growing knot in her head, along with a mug of hot tea.

"I hate to ask this," Maggie said, wrapping her chilled hands around the mug. "But do you have anything stronger? It's not every day that a girl gets mugged."

"I've got just the thing," Tammy replied, and returned a moment later with a bottle of rum from the back room. Clearly, Maggie was in good hands.

Mac and I went out into the snowy street, which was deserted in the winter's twilight. The streetlights had come on as well as the range lights along the canal, filling the old Canal Town with a soft, diffused glow made by the falling snow. Summer was tourist season in our waterfront town, but this time of year, the residents had the town to themselves, which meant that nobody had been on the street to witness the attack. With the snow, most folks had battened down the hatches and hibernated inside, reading or scrolling through Facebook.

However, the storm offered at least one advantage: tracks through the snow. We could see our own tracks, of course, leading from the café steps to the trampled snow surrounding where Maggie had fallen. But three distinct sets of footprints led away from the scene of the mugging.

"Look at that," said Mac, pointing to the tracks in the snow. "All we have to do is follow those footprints. One of these three trails is going to lead to the attacker."

"We have to hurry," I said. "The snow is covering the tracks."

"Hold on," said Mac, and he took out his phone and quickly snapped photos of the three sets of tracks leading away from the scene. He then leaned over the tracks and took close-ups of the individual footprints.

"We'd better split up if we have any hope of following these footprints before the snow covers them," I said. "I'll take these two, and you follow those other tracks."

Mac nodded in agreement. Two sets of footprints moved straight up Bohemia Avenue, almost as if two people had been walking side by side. The third set of prints veered off onto First Street. Mac started heading in that direction.

"Hold on," Mac said, pointing to his assigned tracks. I hadn't noticed before because they were already growing faint under the falling snow, but another small set of footprints ran next to these. I was no tracker, but it looked like these belonged to a dog. "That's either a big dog, or a wolf."

"Seriously? I'm pretty sure that Maggie was not attacked by a wolf."

"Are you sure about that?" asked Mac, looking around at the growing darkness. Shadows grew beyond the circles of soft light cast by the street lamps. Anything could be lurking out there.

"I seriously doubt that a wolf knocked Maggie down and then stole her movie poster."

"Werewolf?" Mac suggested.

"We're wasting time," I said, concerned that within a few minutes the tracks would be gone.

Mac nodded. "Let's just see where these tracks go before they're entirely covered, and then meet back here. Don't go knocking on any doors by yourself. We can go together to where those tracks lead."

"Good idea," I said. Considering that the tracks led to someone who had been violent enough to assault Maggie, it would be a good idea to have Mac around before I confronted any muggers.

We headed our separate ways into the snowy twilight. Covered in snow, the town looked like someone who might be an old friend, but that you weren't quite sure you recognized. I knew Chesapeake City like the back of my hand, having fixed up more than one old house in town for our online home improvement show, *Delmarva Renovators*. I served as the producer and Mac, with his carpentry skills, was the "talent"—his word, not mine. We also had other on-camera crew who explained repairs as well as the care and maintenance required for old houses.

As a kind of sideline, we had also found ourselves solving a murder or two, usually because the crime had interfered with our production schedule. As it turned out, Chesapeake City was the perfect town to use as a base of operations for our show, with lots of history related to the Chesapeake and Delaware Canal, and plenty of old houses to work on.

Quickly, I hurried up the street on my reconnaissance mission. The falling snow threatened to blot out the footprints any minute and they were hard to see anyhow in the dim light. One set of tracks led up the street to the front steps of the C&D Inn. Considering that there were no departing footprints, it was clear that the person had gone inside the inn and not come back out. I made a mental note of that location and followed the second set of prints before they could be lost from view. These brought me directly to the home of Leslie Hammond, who had left the book club early.

Could Leslie be the mugger? I thought about how she had been the first to leave the book club. Maggie described her attacker as a man, but maybe her attacker's winter clothing had confused her. I didn't think Leslie would be much of a threat if I knocked on her door right now, but I had agreed to meet Mac back at the café so that we could talk to these people together—I wasn't quite ready to call them suspects—together rather than taking any chances.

Mission accomplished, I headed back to the café. The street inclined downhill toward the water and I slipped and slid a bit because the pavement was icy under the snow.

Mac was already back at the café, having a stiff drink from the bottle that the café owner had produced. "It's cold out there," he explained, smacking his lips.

"Better give me one, then," I said. Someone handed me a small paper cup into which a shot of rum had been poured. The liquor had a spicy flavor and I could soon feel the warmth spread into my toes and fingertips. It was colder out than I had realized and that wind off the water had a bite.

"My tracks led to Phil Kelly's house," Mac whispered. "You know that Old Man Kelly has that ancient Chesapeake Bay Retriever that he walks through town all the time. I guess those other tracks didn't belong to a wolf, after all."

"The wolf again?" I sighed. "Better have another drink, Mac."

"Don't mind if I do," he said, reaching for the bottle. I noticed that the contents had gone down quite a bit since the bottle had first appeared. Most of the ladies, including Maggie, had telltale paper cups in their hands. This was turning out to be quite a boozy evening for the book club.

I stepped closer to Maggie to get her attention. "Mac and I followed the tracks in the snow that led away from here," I explained. "We're going to go talk to the people at the other end.

Are you sure that you didn't get a look at who attacked you? Any little detail would help."

Maggie shook her head. "It all happened so fast. I just had a glimpse of somebody all bundled up against the cold, and the next thing I knew, I was on the ground and my poster was gone."

The poster itself had shown a still from the movie of actor George Peppard in the cockpit of a World War I fighter plane, goggles down and white silk scarf blowing in the wind, machine guns blazing. Smaller images beneath the plane showed stars Ursula Andress and James Mason in other scenes. The poster was signed by all three of the actors, two of whom had long since shuffled off this mortal stage—thus adding to the value of the poster.

"Any idea how much that poster was worth?" I wondered. I was sure, though, that we weren't talking six figures here. *The Blue Max* was a hit movie in its day but it was not a really famous 1960s classic film like *The Sound of Music* or even something like *Psycho*.

"Well, I've tried to compare it to similar items on eBay," said Maggie. "You know, posters and memorabilia from other films. If you found the right person, I'd say you could get as much as four thousand dollars because the poster is in really good condition and it has a good provenance because it was found in the attic of a home once owned by Jack Hunter."

Hunter, of course, had been the author of *The Blue Max* novel on which the movie was based. Hunter and his wife had moved out of town nearly 30 years ago and must have lost track of the poster at some point.

Maggie ran a shop in town called The Magpie, where she sold antiques and collectibles, so I knew she had a good eye for the prices of things like old movie posters. I wasn't sure that I would have hit someone over the head for four thousand dollars, but people were mugged for less than that every day on the streets of Baltimore and Philadelphia. The question was, who had known that Maggie would happen to be carrying such a valuable autographed poster? Looking around the room, I realized that I was looking at our list of suspects. The thought was unsettling.

"Maybe we should call the Sheriff's Department," Tammy suggested.

Mac spoke up. "I did put in a call," he said. "My source there said to write everything down while it's fresh, but that they were really busy with this storm and would have a hard time getting down here with the roads covered. In other words, we're on our own for now."

It was no secret that Mac's source at the Sheriff's Department was Deputy First Class Maureen Sullivan, whom he had been dating ever since our renovation crew had found a body in the wall while filming work on the Captain Cosden House in town. Chesapeake City was the sort of place where most of the houses in town had names—usually the places were named after long-ago residents. The café, for example, was located in the Cropper House, built back in 1833 as the home of a Chesapeake Bay captain.

Just then the café door was yanked open, filling the room with the smell of snow and fresh air. Leslie Hammond bustled in, brushing snow off her shoulders. It was Leslie who had left the book club early, but now she was back, explaining that the café owner had texted her with news of the attack.

"What on earth happened?" she demanded, her eyes bright with a mixture of concern and what might be excitement. "Maggie, are you all right?"

"I'm pretty shaken up and I've got a nasty bump on my head, but I'll live," Maggie replied. "The worst part is that someone stole my poster."

"Who could have done such a thing?" Leslie wondered.

"I don't know," I said. "But that's what Mac and I are going to find out."

Of course, I had the uncomfortable realization that Leslie herself was a suspect, having left the book club just ahead of

Maggie. Had she lain in wait outside to assault Maggie and steal the poster? Here in the safe confines of the warm café, surrounded by good smells of hot cocoa and coffee and with Leslie hovering in concern, the idea that she had attacked Maggie seemed ridiculous. Still, Mac and I would have to take her aside and ask her a few questions. The sooner, the better.

"Leslie, can I have a word?"

She seemed surprised, but quickly agreed. "Of course."

I led her into the kitchen area of the café with its neatly ordered shelves and stacks of supplies. Mac trailed along and stood in the doorway to block off the kitchen from the rest of the café, giving us some privacy.

"What's all this about?" Leslie asked, although she now sounded annoyed and not as helpful as she had been a minute ago.

"Mac and I found three sets of tracks in the snow leading away from where Maggie was attacked," I explained. "One set of those footprints went directly to your house."

"So? I had to walk up the street to get home."

"You left just a few minutes ahead of Maggie," I said. "Did you see anyone else on the street?"

She thought a moment. "No," she said. Then she frowned. "Wait a minute, Tom. Are you suggesting that I attacked Maggie and stole her silly poster?"

"That 'silly poster' was worth a few thousand dollars," I said. "But I'm not suggesting anything."

"I certainly hope not." Leslie now seemed genuinely angry, her eyes flashing. All of a sudden, it wasn't so hard to picture her giving Maggie a good thump on the head.

For now, I pushed that mental image from my mind. "We were just hoping that you might have seen something. The storm is keeping any deputies from getting down here, so we offered to help."

"Haven't they ever heard of four-wheel drive?" Leslie said.

"Here's a word of advice for you two. Stick with fixing up old houses."

Without another word, she pushed past Mac.

We exchanged a look.

"One down, two to go," Mac said.

"I can hardly wait," I said. "I hope the next couple of conversations go better than that."

OUR NEXT STOP was the home of Old Man Kelly. Mac and I bundled up and headed out into the snow, but not entirely unprepared—Tammy sent us with two cups of hot coffee and a cup of hot cocoa for Mr. Kelly, along with a biscuit for his dog.

Phil Kelly greeted us at the door with a look of surprise. We had bumped into each other often enough around town that we had at least a passing acquaintance. He was clearly relaxing for the evening, wearing baggy wide-wale corduroy trousers, slippers, and a worn fisherman's sweater. Reading glasses were pushed up on his head. An old dog bumped against his knees, wagging his tail but not bothering to bark.

He waved us in and shut the door against the wind and snow. I handed him the hot cocoa and the biscuit for the dog, whose name was Trigger. Deep into his seventies, Old Man Kelly looked fit enough—probably from all those long walks that he took with his dog.

"Tom, Mac, it's good to see you, but I'm a little surprised that you're out in this weather. It's really coming down out there. Is everything all right?"

"It's not, actually," I said, once we were settled in his living room. The house was built in the 1840s using wood from barges dismantled to fit through the old canal locks. A real fire crackled in his fireplace. A big, comfy chair was close enough to the fire to catch the warmth. An open book lay on the floor nearby, along with a bottle of cognac and a small glass. Peering at the title, I could see that it was a copy of Gilbert Byron's *The Lord's Oysters*. All in all, it seemed like the perfect arrangement for a snowy evening.

I almost hated to dispel the pleasant atmosphere in the room by explaining why we were there. "I'm afraid that Maggie Delpino was attacked—mugged—when she left the book club at the café this evening."

It was a little sneaky, but for now I left out the detail about the poster being taken. Mr. Kelly had not been at the book club, so had no way of knowing what had been taken from Maggie.

"Mugged?" He repeated the word as if he couldn't quite understand it, like maybe I wasn't speaking English.

"Hit over the head and shoved so that she fell," I explained.

"That's awful," he said. He shook his head, as if in disbelief. "Thank you for letting me know. I have a bad habit of not locking my doors at night, so I'll be doing that tonight. Old Trigger here isn't much of a watchdog anymore, considering that he's deaf as a post."

"What?" said Mac.

I rolled my eyes at Mac's poor attempt at humor. Mr. Kelly stared at him, then comprehended. "Oh. I get it."

"Actually, why we stopped by, Mr. Kelly, was that we found three sets of tracks leading away from the attack. One set of footprints led us here."

"Really?" He seemed surprised, then smiled. "Why, you're practically a Davy Crockett, aren't you! Following tracks in the snow. Or maybe I should say, a regular Detective Poirot."

Mac spoke up. "What we'd like to know, Mr. Kelly, was whether or not you happened to see anything while you and Trigger were out for a walk."

He thought a moment. "No, no, can't say that we did. Trig and I walked down to the waterfront and then came right back. Our usual route. I brought along my camera and took a few photos of the snow."

"You did?"

"I often bring it along, just in case I spot a ship or something on the canal. I guess it's an old habit. It was getting dark but with the snow I was hoping for a little magic. You see, I worked as a photographer at Aberdeen Proving Ground before I retired."

"May we see the photographs you took tonight?"

"Of course."

He got back out of the chair, his old body cracking with the effort. I had to admit, it seemed unlikely that he had managed to assault Maggie.

To my surprise, he reappeared from the adjoining dining room with a new-looking digital camera that had been sitting on the table there.

He must have caught my look when I saw his high-tech camera. He smiled. "What, were you expecting black and white film, or maybe glass plate negatives? Give me a second to sync this with my laptop over the Bluetooth connection."

Mr. Kelly then located a new MacBook Pro on the coffee table and flipped it open. As promised, the camera downloaded the photos instantly and we were soon peering over his shoulder at snowy scenes along the waterfront.

"Postcard perfect," I said. "You're quite the photographer."

Even Mac grunted in admiration.

"You can see that the streets are quite empty," he said. "Unless—"

"What?" I asked.

"I look a last couple of shots toward the end, looking down the street," he said. "I wonder ... there!"

With a finger, he indicated an image of the snowy downtown, the rectangles of warm yellow light from the buildings and the soft glow of the snow making it all look like something from a Thomas Kincaid painting. However, when I looked more closely at where Mr. Kelly was pointing, there was something more sinister in the photo. It was not obvious at first glance, but a shadowy figure stood against the wall at the corner of the café. It looked for all the world like a mugger lying in wait.

"Who is that?" Mac asked.

"That's got to be the person who attacked Maggie and stole her poster."

"Hold on," Mr. Kelly said. "Stole what poster?"

"Maggie was carrying a poster from *The Blue Max* movie signed by the three famous actors," I explained. "Whoever attacked her didn't bother with Maggie's purse or anything like that. They wanted that poster."

"Sure, I heard about that poster when Maggie found it." Mr. Kelly frowned. "You didn't tell me about the poster because you were testing me. You really are more like Poirot than Davy Crocket!"

"Sorry," I said.

He waved a hand dismissively, then reached for his bottle of cognac. "You boys brought your own coffee, but can I dose it with a little something stronger?"

I declined, but Mac held out his coffee cup for a splash of cognac and Mr. Kelly added some to his hot cocoa as well, humming happily as he did so. When we were all comfortable again, I asked, "Did you know the author when he lived in town?"

"Oh, I knew Jack. He was a very nice man. He and his wife both did a lot for the town before they moved away. Fixed up a couple of houses in town, including the one that's now a B&B. They retired to Florida—considering the weather tonight, maybe they had the right idea."

"Our book club just discussed *The Blue Max* tonight."

The old man nodded. "Jack wrote a good yarn to pass an evening. His character from *The Blue Max* was fairly memorable. Bruno Stachel was a drinker with a flying problem, you might say. The booze was understandable, however, all things considered. Did you know there were no parachutes back then in World War I?"

Dimly, I remembered that detail from reading the book. It must have been a heck of a thing, flying a biplane without a parachute. There was no plan B for those pilots. We finished our coffee, although Old Man Kelly appeared reluctant to let us go, seeming to welcome the company on this lonely night. Finally, we took our leave and headed back into the snowy street.

"What do you think?" I asked Mac.

"Wouldn't hurt a fly," he said. "Who's next?"

———

THE THIRD SET of tracks led to the C&D Inn. By now, several inches of snow covered the roads. No traffic crossed the soaring bridge over the canal and nothing moved on the water. The only sound was the snow sifting into my ears.

Up ahead, lights glowed in the windows of our destination. Built in 1870 by a businessman who had found success renting out mule teams to pull barges through the canal, the grand Victorian-style house was now home to the C&D Inn.

I knocked on the massive, elegantly carved front door and was answered by the innkeeper, Lynn Foster. I was a little surprised that Lynn hadn't joined the book club because she was friends with Maggie Delpino. The two had a lot in common as women who ran businesses in town, catering to the needs of visitors. Both women were about the same age. But where Maggie was dark-haired and dark-eyed, Lynn was light and blond—pale as an Irish milkmaid, in fact.

Her smile beamed at us, warm and welcoming, and she quickly stepped aside so that we could come in. Inside, the inn smelled wonderfully of scones baking or maybe the smell had simply permeated the inn—every guest raved about Lynn's scones.

"Come in out of the cold!" she said. "What are you two doing out on a night like this? Did you have a sudden inspiration to renovate the inn for your show?"

I looked around at the gleaming floors, the original wood-work, and the high ceiling on which was painted a fresco more than a hundred years old. I wasn't sure what other work could be done to such a beautiful place unless Lynn was looking to build an addition. The only thing that looked out of place in this perfectly decorated inn was a pair of boots by the front door, sitting in a puddle of melted snow.

"I'm afraid that Mac and I are here for another reason," I said. "Maggie was assaulted and robbed when she left the book club tonight."

Lynn gasped and put a hand to her chest. If she was acting, then she deserved an Academy Award. "Oh my God! Is Maggie all right?"

"She's shaken up and she got a good bump on the head, but she'll be OK," I said.

Mac's eyes had gone from studying Lynn's reaction to looking out the big windows in the inn's front parlor. Through the wavy glass, we had a clear view of the street and the café beyond, where the attack had taken place. Had Lynn not seen or heard anything?

"You have a good view of the street from here," Mac stated.

"I guess I was in the kitchen baking scones," Lynn said. "You said that Maggie was robbed. I can't imagine that she was carrying enough money to make it worthwhile for a mugger ... a mugger in our little old Canal Town."

"The mugger didn't take money," I explained. "He stole a poster that Maggie was carrying."

Lynn looked puzzled. "A poster? You don't mean that old movie poster she found?"

"One and the same," Mac said. "It seems like everyone in town knew about that poster."

"Word gets around in a small town," Lynn said. "Besides, I was with Maggie that day when she found the poster. We were both helping old Mrs. McCauley clean out her house on George

Street so that her family could sell it and put her into a home. Maggie found that poster up in the attic."

Mac looked pointedly at Lynn. "You must have been disappointed that Maggie found that poster, and not you."

"Whatever do you mean? That poster couldn't have been worth much. Besides, Mrs. McCauley's family let me keep a nice pair of candlesticks. I've got them on the mantel over there. That's the problem, you know—we spend our whole lives accumulating things and then, in the end, we can only keep what fits into a little room in the old folks' home."

I nodded sagely. "There's a lesson in there somewhere," I agreed.

Lynn seemed to remember something, but it turned out only to be her hospitality. "Please make yourselves comfortable. I'll be right back with some scones. And wouldn't you know it, I just made some coffee."

In a minute, she returned with a plate of warm scones, Irish butter, and hot coffee. She placed a cut-glass decanter on the table as well, winking as she did so.

"Delicious," I said, sampling a scone. If I did much more investigating, I would have to go on a diet or maybe join AA.

Mac got right to the point: "It turns out that poster was worth several thousand dollars."

"Really? What a nice surprise for Maggie."

"Lynn, do you have any idea who might have wanted that poster so badly? Are you sure you didn't see or hear anything out on the street?"

She shook her head. "It's just terrible. What is the world coming to when you're not even safe walking at night on Bohemia Avenue?"

I shifted uncomfortably. There was still the matter of the footprints leading to the front porch of the inn, directly from the scene of the attack. If Lynn hadn't made those tracks, then someone had.

"The thing is, we found tracks in the snow leading from the attack to the inn," I said.

Lynn's eyes widened, then sparked angrily. "You don't think— of all the nerve! I even gave you scones! Now, you're saying that I attacked Maggie? I'd like both of you to leave."

Out of the corner of my eye, I saw Mac look down at the tiny plate balanced on his knee, on which sat one of Lynn's famous scones. He seemed to debate what to do with it. Having been ordered out of the inn, was it bad manners to leave with a scone in hand?

"We're here with questions, not accusations," I said, trying to placate Lynn. "Don't you want to know you attacked Maggie?"

"Of course I do, but I can tell you this much—it wasn't me! Now, please go!"

Beside me, Mac had arrived at a solution to the scone question. He reached for the golden brown scone on his plate with a hand the size of a paw and wolfed it down in three bites. We stood to go, but I wasn't quite ready to abandon ship.

"We're just trying to get to the bottom of this, Lynn."

"I understand that, Tom, but coming here and accusing me of attacking my best friend in town isn't doing much good finding the attacker, is it?"

"Listen, just bear with me for a minute, and then we'll go. If those were not *your* footprints leading to your porch, then whose might they be?" I asked. "I saw a pair of boots by the front door when we came in. Whose are those?"

"Like I said, I haven't been out." Lynn's eyes widened all over again. "Wait, I do have a guest here, a Mr. Applebaum. You don't think—"

"What I think is that we should talk to Mr. Applebaum. Would you mind getting him?"

"Of course not. I'll be right back. I'm sorry if I lost my temper. I know you're just trying to help, but it's not easy being accused of something like that. Please, help yourselves to more scones while I'm gone."

Lynn disappeared up the sweeping staircase, and Mac reached happily for the plate of scones. "We may or may not figure out who attacked Maggie," he said. "But we *are* going to be well-fed."

"Something doesn't add up," I said. "There were three sets of footprints leading away from the scene of the attack. One set of those footprints must lead to the attacker. If we cross Leslie Hammond and Old Man Kelly of our list, that leaves this guy Applebaum."

"It's got to be him, then. Don't worry, I'll make sure that he doesn't make a run for it."

"Better keep your energy levels up, just in case. You might need another scone."

"Good idea," Mac said, and reached for the plate.

A few minutes later, Lynn returned, leading her guest into the room. At first glance, Applebaum didn't look like a mugger. He was forty-something, of average height and a bit pudgy through the middle, with neatly cut graying hair and rimless executive-style eyeglasses. He padded across the floor in navy blue dress socks that had little anchors on them. All in all, he looked less like a mugger than a businessman, which is just what he turned out to be.

"I'm Vince Applebaum," he said, quickly pumping our hands with his firm handshake. "Lynn has explained the situation. Something about a mugging across the street? That's just awful in this little town. I don't know how I can help, but I'd be happy to give you any sort of statement you need."

"They're not the police," Lynn pointed out. "They're renovators."

Now Applebaum looked confused. "Renovators?"

"This is totally unofficial," I explained. "But we've had some experience in this area before and with the weather, the sheriff's office asked us to gather some evidence before it was all buried in the snow."

"Makes sense," Applebaum said, although the look on his face said otherwise.

"Have a scone," Lynn said to him.

"Don't mind if I do."

Once we all get settled again on the parlor furniture with our coffee cups and scones, I asked the inn's lone guest, "What brings you to Chesapeake City, Mr. Applebaum?"

"Business," he said. "I work for an investment group that's looking to expand its holdings and there's a marina in the area that we're looking to buy."

"Who shops for marinas in the middle of winter?" Mac asked, sounding skeptical.

"It's actually the perfect time," Applebaum said. "Once the weather breaks, we can have everything up and running under our new management team and get started with any infrastructure improvements that we have planned. The inn is quite convenient and a lot better than a hotel off the interstate."

"Have you been out tonight, Mr. Applebaum?" Mac asked, cutting to the chase once more. "Maybe you decided to take a little stroll in the snow?"

"No," he said. "I've been up in my room all evening, crunching some numbers from the marina's books."

"Then can you tell me why your boots are sitting by the front door in a puddle of melted snow?"

Applebaum turned and looked toward the front door, where that pair of boots did indeed sit in a widening puddle of water. I began to worry about damage to the floor, but that was the renovator in me.

"Those are my snow boots," Applebaum agreed. "I brought them along when I heard the weather forecast. But like I said, I haven't been out in the snow. I have no idea how those boots got there."

"Is that so?" Mac said doubtfully. "There's one way that we can tell for sure."

"And how is that?" Applebaum wondered. "Look, if you

people are from the marina's neighbors or something, I can assure you that we aren't planning—"

"That's not it at all, Mr. Applebaum," Mac said, moving into bad cop mode. "We know all about you and *The Blue Max*, don't we?"

"*The Blue Max*? You mean that old movie? What on earth are you talking about?"

"Come with me, Mr. Applebaum." Mac stood up, looking huge even beneath the high ceilings. The way that he said the words was more of an order than an invitation. Reluctantly, Applebaum stood. Actually, we all did, and followed Mac over to the wet boots. He picked them up and looked at the soles. The boots were still wet, which made the pattern of the treads easy to see. Mac then took out his phone. "Let's compare, shall we? I took pictures of the footprints before the snow covered them up. If the treads match, we've got a winner."

Mac held up his phone, and he scrolled through the photos he had taken of the footprints, each showing the unique tread marks pressed into the snow by the owner's boots. To our surprise, none of the treads in the photos matched those of Applebaum's boots.

"Well, I guess that proves it," Applebaum said. "Let's all sit down and have some more scones."

"But those *are* his boots by the front door!" Lynn insisted. "You can tell that he's been out!"

Lynn had a point. I was as confused as the others. It just made sense that Applebaum's boots should match those in the pictures. If the footprints led to the inn, the attacker had not simply vanished.

Mac spoke up: "Tom, take a look in the hall closet, will you?"

Lynn tried to get between me and the closet, but I dodged around her. She said, "It's such a mess in there. There's no need—"

Ignoring her, I opened the hall closet, which was packed with winter coats, umbrellas, and a vacuum cleaner tucked into one corner. There were also several pairs of shoes and boots—one of which sat in its own puddle of melted snow.

"Huh," I said.

"Let's have a look at the tread of those boots, shall we?" Mac suggested.

I held up the boots from the closet, and Mac produced his phone again. Sure enough, the pictures of the treads from the footprints leading to the inn matched the treads on the bottom of these boots.

"I think we can all agree that we have a winner," Mac said.

"Sure, they match," Applebaum stated in his matter-of-fact businessman manner. "But whose boots are they?"

Lynn went back into the parlor and sat down on the sofa. She put her face in her hands. Her shoulders began to shake, and it didn't take a detective to realize that she was sobbing.

Us three men looked on uncomfortably. Any one of us would have preferred it if Lynn had started waving around a loaded revolver or a butcher knife. That, we could handle. With tears, she had gone nuclear on us.

Working up our nerve, we edged back into the parlor. "Lynn," I said softly. "Want to explain what all this is about?"

Finally, she lowered her hands, revealing puffy eyes and a face streaked with tears. Lynn was an attractive woman, but she seemed to have aged ten years in as many minutes. "I did it, OK? Maggie told me that she was going to be at the book club with the poster tonight. With this storm, I thought that I could get the poster away from her once she was alone in the street and nobody would be the wiser. I'm an awful person."

"But why?"

She sniffed. "Maggie and I were working cleaning out Mrs. McCauley's house, which you already know. When Maggie found that poster up in the attic, I didn't much care at the time, but she didn't offer to share it with me or anything. Her attitude was more like, finder's keepers. Come to find out, that old movie poster was worth a few thousand dollars. Not a fortune, I know, but wouldn't it have been nice if Maggie offered to share it with me? If I had found the poster, that's what I would have done for her."

"Lynn, it's a few thousand dollars. It's not a fortune."

"I know, I know," she moaned. "But things haven't been all that great business-wise. With all the rain last summer, I had a lot of vacancies. Then the furnace went up and I had to replace that. Ten thousand dollars just like that! For what that poster is worth, I can keep going until the new season and hopefully have a chance at a busy summer."

"I'm sorry that you were in that situation, but I don't see how mugging your friend was much of a solution."

"What can I say?" Lynn wailed, "I'm a monster!"

"If you had hit Maggie a little harder or if she had fallen and hit her head, then you might be a murderer. Let's just be glad that this is as far as things went."

Mac said, "Maybe Applebaum here could buy you out—"

"Hey—"

"You're not helping, you two," I said. "Mr. Applebaum, go get a glass of water for Lynn, please. Mac, you'd better text those pictures to your sheriff's department friend."

"Am I going to jail?" Lynn asked.

"Not tonight," I said. "The roads are a mess. I think you can stay right here."

Lynn smiled ruefully. "The inn that I broke the law to save becomes my prison."

"That's one way to look at it," I said. "Sometimes, we make bad choices to protect the things we love."

Across the street, lights shone brightly in the window of the café, still abuzz with tonight's events. In some sense, the café had been ground zero tonight for everything that had happened, truly the house that brewed up trouble.

"I should go across the street and apologize to Maggie," Lynn said.

"Somehow, I don't think that would be a good idea right now. There will be time for that later."

"Maybe you're right.

"Where is the poster, by the way?"

"In the closet, hidden behind the vacuum cleaner."

Mac and I had solved the crime and caught Maggie's attacker —but I didn't feel so great about it. Lynn would likely be arrested. Even if Maggie didn't press charges, at the very least, Lynn couldn't expect to keep her business going—the court of public opinion delivered justice too swiftly and directly.

Tonight's events raised several uncomfortable questions. How far would we go to save our livelihoods? Who among us hasn't been envious? Had Maggie been wrong to claim the valuable poster all for herself? Are the bonds of friendship and community stronger than the pull of money or envy? How well do we truly know our friends?

Beyond the windows of the old inn, snow continued to fall fast and deep. I would have liked to say that the residents of the old Canal Town could have slept easier that night, knowing that Maggie Delpino's attacker had been caught, but the cold wind off the canal rattled the window frames and made the old houses creak uneasily, promising a fretful night filled with soul searching.

LEGAL ISSUES

"We've got trouble," Reggie said. He had burst through the door and was standing now in the cramped law office, the fat under his chin trembling and beads of sweat wetting his upper lip. "Geez, Zach, you should have seen it."

"What?" Zach crumpled another sheet of paper from the yellow legal pad and looped it toward the wastebasket. The wadded paper circled the rim and fell in.

"That guy just blew Bill away. Bang." Reggie's whole body quaked and his face turned fish-belly white. He bolted for the bathroom and Zach heard him retching. Zach shook his head.

Reggie never did have the stomach for being a good lawyer, Zach thought. Zach sighed, crumpled another sheet of paper and shot it toward the wastebasket. He watched it swoosh in, then got up and filled a glass with water.

Reggie came back out, wiping his face with a brown paper towel.

"Sit down and tell me about it," Zach said, handing Reggie the water. The other man's hand shook as he took a drink.

"Well, there we were, going on up to this guy's front door to serve him a termination order, right? No big deal. It's a nice neighborhood off River Road; we're not expecting anything.

Hell, Bill is telling me about the trip he and his wife took to Williamsburg over the weekend. Next thing I know the front door opens, the guy has a gun and he just blows Bill away."

"He didn't fire at you?"

"No, he just shut the door easy-as-you-please. And there's Bill, his eyes wide open, laying on his back—"

"Easy, Reggie, easy. Who the hell was this guy?"

"His name was George Brennan. Routine termination order is all."

"Who's bringing the order against him?"

"Just some guy Brennan clipped in a car accident. His car skidded in that big snowstorm we got in February and they kissed bumpers. Nobody even got hurt. But this other guy thought he could get some money out of it."

"What kind of gun was it?"

"Some sort of shotgun, I'd say. I'm not a gun guy, Zach, you know that. I'm not that kind of lawyer."

"What did the police say?" Zach asked. "Did they arrest the guy?"

"That's the hell of it. You know the law as well as I do. Because we were lawyers, serving a termination order, they said the guy had a perfect legal right to shoot Bill."

"But we hadn't served the papers yet!"

"That's what I told the cops. And they said, 'But your intent was to serve a termination order, right?' " So, of course, I said yes. And they said the guy had every right to blow Bill away. Self-defense. Jesus."

Zach left Reggie sipping his glass of water and went over to look out the glass door of the office into the street. The letters painted on the glass were backwards from inside, but Zach knew them well enough: Taylor, Downs & Feinstein. Attorneys at law. He and Bill Downs had started the firm back in the days when lawyers first went into the termination business. In those early years, he and Bill had sometimes carried out as many as one termination order a week. It had been a bloody business for a while. Reggie Feinstein joined later, when the profession had settled upon a system, and nobody got killed anymore. Or at least, not very often. Bill's being shot was a case in point.

Termination orders had come about because lawsuits had become so commonplace that the courts were swamped. Then, the U.S. Supreme Court, in a fit of conservative, eye-for-an-eye righteousness, decided it was all right in certain cases for a plaintiff and defendant to use deadly force to settle their differences.

The lawyers jumped right in. Zach and Bill were one of the first to go into the business. Quickly, the lawyers worked out a system.

Say some guy lost his leg in a car accident. He's angry because the driver who hit him was drunk. It would take years for the lawsuit to slog its way through the courts. So the injured party hires an attorney to carry out a termination order. The drunken driver is served notice that he's going to be gunned down. Well, that driver and his family are going to be running scared, so they hire an attorney to protect his rights. He's now got himself a bodyguard and counter-terminator who can go after the injured party. Both attorneys get a fee from their prospective clients and the drunken driver pays up some kind of settlement to get the termination order off his back.

Nobody got killed anymore, and attorneys made a living. Some do-it-yourselfers opted to fight an old-fashioned duel and save on the legal fees, but most people preferred professional advice. That way, nobody got hurt.

"We've got to get this guy," Zach said, the old steel coming into his voice. "This is going to end up on the news, and if people start getting the idea that they can settle their own termination orders, it's going to put a lot lawyers out of work. We can't have that. The state bar association will not be happy."

"He's a nut, Zach, I'm telling you. He was just as calm as could be when he was talking to the cops afterwards. He told them he was so sorry to cause so much trouble for them, that he knew they had better things to do, like catch rapists." Reggie's voice began to tremble again. "And you know what?"

"No. What?" Zach was trying to imagine what could be worse than being compared to a rapist.

"He told the cops a joke."

"Yeah?"

"He said, 'How do you tell the difference between lawyer road kill and dog road kill?' "

When Reggie didn't supply the punch line, Zach sighed and said, "I give up, Reggie. How do you tell?"

"There's skid marks in front of the dog.'"

Zach shook his head. His old friend Bill had become the punchline to a lawyer joke. It wasn't right. "Jesus. This guy has got an attitude."

"The cops laughed, Zach! It made me shake all over. There was poor Bill being zipped into a body bag and the cops are laughing at lawyer jokes."

Zach went over to the weapons cabinet and took out his favorite sawed-off shotgun. He stood for a moment, admiring the deep blue-black barrel and the nicks in the gunstock. Those gouges and scratches came from hard use in the early days. The mere sight of the gun and the sound of a shell being racked into the chamber were enough to settle most disputes. "Habeus Corpus" was his nickname for the 12-gauge. The magazine held five shells and he alternated them as he loaded the shotgun, double "O" buckshot to take a man down or shred a door, followed by a rifled slug that could stop the most belligerent defendant or plaintiff.

Zach handed Reggie a Ruger P-85 handgun. The sleek 9 mm automatic wasn't as mean-looking as the shotgun, but it was good enough for close work. Besides, he knew that Reggie couldn't shoot worth a damn.

"Come on Reggie, we've got work to do. Bring that file on George Brennan. We can read it in the car. We need to find a way to crack this nut."

ZACH DROVE FASTER than he should have, his hands tight on the wheel. People said the law was boring, but at the moment he was looking forward to delivering some justice.

They arrived in a modest neighborhood of well-kept houses. Like every other house on the block, George Brennan's place was a three-bedroom split-level with a narrow strip of yard separating it from the identical houses on each side. Brennan had evidently taken some pride of ownership, though, planting a nice specimen of a Japanese maple in the front yard.

There was no sign of Brennan, however, and no car in the driveway. Most people seemed to be at work. An old lady came by walking her dog, giving them the stink eye. Two guys sitting in a car all day did seem suspicious. Afternoon slipped toward evening, and they continued to wait down the street in the aging Tesla they used for surveillance. Reggie put the seat back and took a nap.

Zach used the last of the daylight to read Brennan's file as he sipped coffee from a foam cup. "He's been divorced twice. His wives' attorneys took him to the cleaners both times, from the looks of it. Used to have a place at the beach. He second wife got that."

"Ouch," Reggie said.

"And get a load of this, Reggie. Ours is the third termination order that's been brought against him. The first was from his first wife. He paid up, it seems. The second order was a neighbor at the beach property. Something about a fence being over the property line....Oh boy."

"What?"

"He went to the attorney's office and broke both the guy's legs. The termination order was dropped."

Reggie sat up and grabbed the dashboard. "This is just great, Zach. We're dealing with a real psycho. He goes around breaking some poor attorney's legs over a termination order? Doesn't he know how it works? Everybody reaches a settlement these days and nobody gets hurt." Reggie buckled his seatbelt, which he had undone for his nap. "It's over, Zach. Start driving. Let's get out of here."

Zach made no move to start the car. He turned and stared at Reggie with his best courtroom glare. "You want to run, Reggie? This joker killed Bill. We've got to get him. We're going to carry out this termination order. With extreme prejudice. It's the only thing to do."

"All right." Reggie sighed, resigned to his fate. "Three years of law school for this. Whatever happened to the good old days when all lawyers did was file papers, make a few phone calls, meet with clients, and charge two hundred bucks an hour?"

"You know what happened as well as I do. There got to be too many of us wanting the two hundred bucks an hour and not enough people around to pay it."

Ignoring Reggie, Zach continued reading. What he read next nearly made him spill the rest of his coffee. He sat up with a jolt.

"What?" Reggie asked.

"Nothing." Zach decided that it wasn't something he was going to share with Reggie. His law partner was jumpy enough already. He kept reading, wishing that Bill had done his due diligence before confront Brennan. No wonder the guy was a hothead. Bill might have taken some precautions if he'd read more than Brennan's address on the termination order.

According to the file, Brennan was an attorney who had been disbarred years ago for being overzealous in carrying out termination orders. Turned out that he liked shooting people. Nothing was worse than taking on one of your own kind.

BRENNAN RETURNED HOME JUST before dark, driving one of those monstrous old gas-guzzling SUVs. The only people who still drove those were the ones who couldn't afford a newer electric vehicle—or people who preferred the roar of a V-8.

He didn't stay long, but went out again. Zach tailed him with the Tesla, trailing in the wake of noxious combustion fumes. Brennan drove so fast that he was hard to keep up with in the evening traffic.

From the passenger seat, Reggie watched the SUV intently. He pointed and said, "He's turning into that fast food place."

"All right. I see him. Take the safety off that Ruger."

"We're going to hit him here?" Reggie asked.

"Yeah. This place is as good as any. If we're lucky, we'll catch him by surprise."

Reluctantly, Zach left the 12-gauge behind. The shotgun was too obvious to lug into the fast food joint without sending everyone into a panic, so they would have to rely on Reggie's automatic.

Zach thought about taking the Ruger from Reggie, but decided against it. He had given his partner the gun so Reggie could carry out at least one actual termination order during his career. Zach had done his share back in the day. It was time for Reggie to man up.

When Reggie saw that Zach had left the shotgun, he tried to give him the pistol.

"You hang onto that," Zach said.

"You want *me* to shoot him?"

"You'll thank me later."

Reggie took a seat at the back of the restaurant as Zach went to order sodas and burgers. The place was kind of old and run down, like it had been remodeled on the cheap one time too many. The owners had cut corners by leaving in the old light fixtures and tired floor tiles.

He kept an eye on Brennan, who was in line just ahead of him. Brennan was a little under six feet, solidly built like he might have played football or wrestled back in high school, and wearing a rumpled off-the-rack suit that still made him look like a lawyer. He was otherwise unremarkable, just another lonely divorced guy grabbing something to eat.

The man didn't know him, so Zach didn't worry about being recognized. Brennan took his time ordering, reading through the menu, then waited patiently for his order as if he didn't have a care in the world. Zach felt even more confident that his plan would work when he saw the extra-large soda on Brennan's tray. The man walked past him and sat down, not giving Zach so much as a glance.

Zach got his own order and rejoined Reggie. Zach noticed that Reggie had shredded several paper napkins in his absence, the remains of which were now scattered around the table like confetti. Without anything to keep them busy, Reggie's hands were shaking. Zach hoped those hands would be steady enough to hit someone at point-blank range with a 9 mm.

"Now what?" Reggie asked anxiously when Zach sat down with the food.

"Eat," Zach said. "It's been a long day. Aren't you hungry?"

"You're serious, aren't you?" Reggie stared at him, then proceeded to push French fries around his tray.

"Ketchup?" Zach asked, holding up a packet. He tore it open and squeezed the red glop onto his own tray.

Reggie blanched at the sight of the ketchup. He pushed his food away, uneaten.

Zach ate, casting sideways glances at Brennan. Reggie had been careful to keep his back to the man so he wouldn't be recognized. Brennan finished, dumped his tray, and started toward the restroom. So far, everything was going according to plan.

Zach had kept his eye on the restroom door and knew Brennan was alone in there. If someone else had gone in, Zach would have called it off. Things got messy when there were bystanders involved. No sense killing more people than they had to. They were lawyers, not murderers.

"Action," Zach said. "Slip your hand inside your jacket and check the gun. Is the safety off?"

Reggie had been chewing on some ice from his soda. He swallowed hard. "Yeah," Reggie croaked.

Zach slid the termination order across the table. "Put this in your pocket to keep everything nice and legal. Go in the restroom. Brennan will be taking a leak. You walk in with the gun out and say, 'Mr. George Brennan?' When he turns around, let him have it. Nothing fancy. Two in the chest."

Reggie nodded. "Yeah. OK."

"One more thing," Zach said. He leaned across the plastic table and tapped the document. "And it's the best part. After you shoot him, roll this termination order into a little tube and stick it in his mouth. It'll be a nice touch. Sends the appropriate message."

"OK." Reggie sat as if awaiting further instructions. "That's it?"

"That's it. Now go."

Reggie put the termination order in his pocket, then stood up and hurried toward the restroom. He pulled on the door, not realizing that he had to push it open. He figured it out and slipped inside.

Zach kept his head cocked toward the door, waiting for the boom of the Ruger. Nothing. Twenty seconds went by. Thirty. A full minute. Nervous as Reggie had been, it still shouldn't have taken him that long to figure out how to pull the trigger. What the hell was going on?

Then Brennan walked out with one hand in the pocket of his suit. Zach was certain that hand would be holding Reggie's gun.

Brennan stopped near the door and looked around, taking his time, trying to pick out any more attorneys. There were a few other men in suits and ties, and Zach hoped that he blended in.

Brennan's eyes slithered over the diners. Zach was acutely aware of the naked spot under his armpit where a shoulder holster should have been, and he cursed his own confidence.

Zach pretended to be checking his phone, a cup of soda within reach. Maybe Brennan wouldn't notice that there were two trays on the table.

Zach chanced a look in Brennan's direction. Brennan was staring at him, one hand still stuck in his pocket. The hand holding the pistol. Maybe a pistol that was aimed in Zach's direction. Brennan smiled at Zach and slipped out the door.

Zach jumped up and ran for the restroom.

He stiff-armed the door open and found Reggie face down on the cold tile floor. His partner's eyes bulged like two peeled, hard-boiled eggs and his face had a purplish tint like bruised fruit. You didn't have to be an expert to know that Reggie was dead. A major clue was the fact that one side of Reggie's skull had been crushed like an egg shell.

On the floor nearby was the lid from a toilet tank. That bastard Brennan must have spotted one or both attorneys in the joint, figured out what was going on, and grabbed the porcelain lid as a weapon.

Zach saw it all clearly because it was the same thing he would have done in Brennan's shoes. When Reggie walked in with his gun out, Brennan would have been standing to one side of the wall, out of sight, and then he had stepped up behind Reggie and taken him out. The lid weighed a good ten pounds but Brennan was the kind of guy who had some heft to him. One good whack was all it took.

Zach had to give Brennan credit. The guy had caught on that he was being followed. Zach had figured that Brennan would walk right into their trap, but the guy had been one step ahead, setting a trap of his own. The guy was good, too damn good, and the thought made Zach nervous.

Zach knelt on the floor and gave Reggie's shoulder a quick squeeze as if to reassure him. Not that Reggie could feel it, but it made Zach feel better. Then he walked out of the restroom, leaving someone else to find Reggie's body and call the police to clean up the mess. The termination order gripped in Reggie's dead hand would let them know that this hadn't been a simple murder.

Zach walked out of the fast food joint, vowing that he wasn't about to give up. This was no longer about professional pride. Bill and Reggie were dead. There was a lot more at stake here. This was personal.

He took a good look around the parking lot before walking to the car, but Brennan was nowhere in sight. He got the shotgun out of the trunk and set it on the empty passenger seat, which was still tilted back from Reggie's nap earlier.

If Zach was sure of anything, he was sure that George Brennan was as good as dead.

THE NEXT MORNING, Zach was sitting at his desk in the office having a cup of coffee and trying to figure out what to do next. To help the process along, he had dosed his coffee with a bottle of Tullamore Dew that he kept in his bottom desk drawer. For security, he had an old police-issue .38 special revolver on the blotter in front of him. The pistol was practically an antique, but Brennan had disappeared with the P-85 that Reggie had been carrying.

That wasn't Zach's only weapon, though. The middle drawer of the old wooden desk was just long enough for him to wedge the sawed-off shotgun inside. The drawer was open, and all Zach had to do was reach down and pull the trigger to unleash a handful of buckshot that would blow away anyone standing in front of the desk. It was a trick from the early days: keep a decoy gun out where everyone could see it, then keep your ace-in-the-hole gun someplace they couldn't.

He was staring through the glass door with the name sof his dead partners on it, trying to figure out what to do next, when the glass exploded. He shut his eyes in time to keep from being blinded by the swarming, jagged shards.

He felt the next blast punch several holes in him before he could roll to the floor. A third blast blew the doorknob and double bolt off the door. Two more shots came through the open doorway, just to clear the room. Some part of Zach's mind managed to appreciate the technique involved.

From the floor, Zach watched his desktop computer die in a shower of sparks. It fell to the floor, smoking and stinking of burned wiring. His coffee mug shattered and his framed law degree slipped to the floor like a wing-shot bird.

Zach briefly gave in to his urge to curl up in a ball and pray. Once the shooting stopped, though, he snapped out of it. He knew he only had a few seconds to set the stage. He forced himself to move.

Any good lawyer also needed to be a good actor. But Zach didn't need to convince a jury—he just needed to convince the man who was gunning for him.

Zach grabbed the old revolver off the desk and tossed it on the floor a few feet away. He was in the process of reaching for it when Brennan walked in with the Ruger drawn and pointed at Zach.

"I wouldn't do that if I were you," Brennan warned. "If you go for that gun, I'm going to take my time killing you."

"You win," Zach said, slumping against the side of the desk. His body language reeked of defeat.

"I waited for you all night at my place," Brennan said. "I figured you'd make a run at me, but I guess I figured wrong. We can't just leave this business unfinished. Somebody needed to have some balls, so I finally decided to pay you an office visit."

"Maybe we can talk about this," Zach said, putting a pleading note in his voice. It wasn't hard to do. He gazed covetously at the revolver a few feet away on the floor.

"What do you want me to do? Let you go?"

"Sure," Zach said. "We could just let the statute of limitations run out. Technically, we've reached a settlement."

Brennan laughed. "Nice try. But I can't let you go—some day

I'll step out my front door and there you'll be. You're just like me, a lawyer from the old days. We don't give up. It's too bad we didn't have a chance at the courtroom when we began our careers. We would have been unbeatable trial attorneys. Civil suits. Defense for drug kingpins. Think of the money! But there were too many of us already and we had to make a living some-how, so we went into the termination business."

"Even lawyers have to eat," Zach said. He jostled himself slightly, ignoring the pain and his leaking blood as he shifted closer to the revolver.

"You want that gun, don't you?" Brennan said. "See what I mean about not giving up?"

"Just let me reach for it, get it in my hand. Don't make me die like this."

"Professional courtesy?"

"Yeah."

Brennan seemed to consider the idea. The Ruger never wavered, but remained pointed squarely at Zach. Finally, Brennan said, "I'm sure as hell not going to let you get a loaded gun in your hand. Tell you what. I'll dump out the cylinder and then kick it over to you. It'll only be a prop, but ..." Brennan shrugged, indicating that it was the best he could do.

"Jesus, anything," Zach pleaded. "Just don't make me look like a coward."

Brennan chuckled, shook his head, and stooped to pick up the revolver, keeping his own gun trained in Zach's direction. Brennan was no more than six feet from the front of the desk, standing right in the kill zone. Playing his part, Zach held one hand out to receive his empty revolver in his right hand. He left hand crept unnoticed into the open drawer of his shattered desk, closed around the trigger of the shotgun, and gave it a yank.

Splinters of flying wood and buckshot erupted from the desk, peppering Brennan's suit jacket and white shirt with jagged holes. Brennan staggered, somehow managing to stay on his feet. He blinked rapidly, then finally stared at Zach as the knowledge of what had happened filled his eyes with a helpless, dying rage. Then the light faded from Brennan's eyes. He was dead before he hit the floor.

Zach finally breathed again. His face burned where it had been raked by the glass shards from the door, and he had forgotten how much it hurt to be shot back in the bad, old days. But the buckshot hadn't hit anything serious. He could move, and his wounds didn't leak too badly when he pulled himself up and back into his chair.

Right now his body was numb, but in a few minutes he knew from experience that he would begin to feel screaming pain as a million raw nerve endings protested being so rudely traumatized. The bottle of Irish whiskey had somehow survived in the bottom desk drawer and he took a pull to help take the edge off the coming pain.

Lawyers were a bad bunch, all right, but at least he understood them. He was one of them, after all. But a lawyer wouldn't be able to patch up his wounds. Zach fumbled for the phone. He hated to do it, but he knew he had to get some help from somebody that he trusted even less than a lawyer. He sighed. And called a doctor.

SEEKER

My mind is elsewhere as I watch the blade of my circular saw rip another sheet of plywood. The spinning blade makes me wonder about the nature of sin and forgiveness and how it's an endless cycle. Then I push any stray thoughts out of my head and pay attention to the whirring blade.

It's a tricky cut, a thirty-inch run and then a ninety-degree angle, which is why I'm doing it because I'm the best craftsman on the crew. The blade bucks at the shift in the grain and a blizzard of sawdust whirls always in the breeze. I have to stop, back up, move around the sheet of plywood and come at the thick pencil line from another angle.

I'm in the middle of what used to be a soybean field in Delaware, putting up one of the houses in a development to be known as Drawyers Creek Estates. These days, most houses arrive on the back of a truck in modular sections and we lift the walls into place with the rough openings for windows and doors already framed in. But they haven't figured everything out at the factory, which is why they still need a man who can measure and cut.

We quit for lunch and I find some shade inside the skeleton of the house. Most of my co-workers are Mexicans who sit

outside in a semi-circle on a patch of grass, laughing and chat-
tering away. I know enough Spanish to catch about every third
or fourth word.

Framing houses is grunt work for the most part. There are
only a couple of other guys on the crew who aren't Mexican.
They sit apart in the shade of a pickup truck, listening to
country music on the radio. One starts drinking as soon as he
gets in his truck at the end of the day and the other steals whatever he can when the foreman isn't looking. I'm not that friendly
with either of them.

I've brought along a newspaper and scan the national news
on Page 6. Gas prices going up. Rattling the saber over North
Korea. And in Connecticut, a twelve-year-old girl is missing,
snatched on her way home from school. I finish my lunch and go
back to work early. The Mexicans give me a look that doesn't
need translation, then ignore me as I start swinging the framing
hammer, hitting the nails so hard that each blow echoes like a
gunshot.

The sun is going down when we call it quits. It's Friday,
payday, so I cash my check, and then stop at a library on the way
home. I sign up for an hour of computer time and spend it
reading everything I can about the missing girl. There are no
suspects, but police say it's similar to a case from a year ago. And
another from a year before that. The bodies of both those other
girls turned up by the side of the road, wrapped in plastic sheet-
ing. I try not to think about that too much. The last thing I do is
print out a map.

I've been staying at a motel bordering a state highway. Most
of the units are long-term rentals for construction workers and
the parking lot is almost deserted on a Friday evening because
anyone who's got a real home to go to has headed there for the
weekend. I shower and change into clean clothes: worn jeans,
and a T-shirt. It doesn't take me long to get my things together.
My clothes fill a cardboard box. I toss a couple of books on top.
The last thing I pack is a picture frame, which I wrap carefully

in bubble wrap before tucking it deep into the box of clothes. We had that family portrait taken at a J.C. Penny a few weeks before Christmas, about a year before my wife died of cancer.

Other than what I've spent on food and rent, I have almost all my wages from the last six months, which amounts to just over six thousand dollars, and I tuck as much as I can into an old-fashioned money belt, then put the rest in an envelope that goes into the cardboard box.

It's not even eight p.m. when I slide into bed and set the alarm for midnight. Before I fall asleep, I turn those questions in my mind like I have a thousand times before: does one evil outweigh another? Can sin truly be forgiven? They click together with a sound like rosary beads as the digital eye of the alarm clock stares. At some point I manage to fall asleep, tired from a long day slapping houses together, because the next thing I hear is the alarm going off.

Before I walk out, I take one last look to make sure I haven't forgotten anything. Other than the rumpled bed, there's no sign I've been living in this room for months. It's a reassuring thought that I can come and go now without even being noticed. I turn off the light and start up my truck.

Connecticut is a six-hour drive. There's almost nobody else on the road and the radio stations drift in and out with the miles. Emily keeps me company. She sits in the passenger seat and looks out the window, listening to the music with me. The Who. Rolling Stones. U-2. Good driving songs. She's still wearing her swimsuit with an oversize sweatshirt to keep her warm, her eight-year old body still pudgy with baby fat. When I stop for coffee she's gone by the time I come back out. A few minutes later, crossing the Tappan Zee Bridge, daybreak is touching the Hudson River. I can't look out at the water but keep my eyes on the road.

A couple of hours later, I show up at the house with a stack of fliers and a box of doughnuts. It's a Tudor-style house, not much bigger than a cottage. The flagstone sidewalk is lined with landscape lights and some geraniums are blooming in a pot on the front step.

"Can I help you?" asks the guy who answers the door. He's big and he stands in the doorway, blocking it. He looks forty-something, short hair going bald on top.

"I've been reading about what happened." I hold out the box of doughnuts. "I'd like to help."

He eyes the doughnuts, then looks me over. "It's all in the hands of the police right now. We haven't really organized any volunteers—"

"Who is it, Bill?" comes a woman's voice from deeper in the house.

Bill half-turns to call back, "Some guy who want to help."

"He's not a reporter, is he?"

Keeping his eyes on me, Bill shouts back into the house, "He doesn't look like one."

"Well, let him in."

Bill hesitates, then shrugs and steps aside. I hand him the doughnuts and walk in. The front door opens directly into the living room, where a candle smelling of cinnamon burns in front of a framed picture of the missing girl. Voices hum in the kitchen, where several people are gathered, friends and neighbors mostly, would be my guess. They nod hello.

"He brought doughnuts," Bill announces.

"That was nice," says the woman sitting at the table. From her voice, I know it's the same person who told Bill to let me in. Her eyes are rimmed red and her chestnut hair is tousled. At first glance, she looks to be in her forties. This must be Jenna's mom.

"I also brought fliers," I say, setting the stack down on the table. "I hope you don't mind."

The woman picks one up and studies it. I made up the flier at the library yesterday afternoon and stopped that morning to make color copies. There's a large photograph of Jenna taken off a website, a picture showing a smiling young girl with hair like her mother's. MISSING it says at the very top of the page in bold type. Beneath the photograph is Jenna's full name and physical description. JENNA DISAPPEARED WHILE WALKING HOME FROM SCHOOL ON TUESDAY, SEPTEMBER 20. IF YOU HAVE SEEN ANYTHING THAT MIGHT HELP FIND JENNA, PLEASE CALL POLICE. There's the number for a police hotline at the bottom.

She looks at the flier a long time, sniffles and swipes at her nose, then gets up and uses a magnet to put a flier on the refrigerator. "These are very good," she says, then introduces herself as Claire after she thanks me for the fliers. "We should put these around town right away." Two or three people move to obey as if she were a general giving orders.

"I've got a staple gun in my truck," I say. "You should probably start by putting them up along the most likely route Jenna would have taken home from school. After that, I would start putting them in gas stations, convenience stores, the post office, wherever people come and go."

"You sure seem to know a lot about it," says Bill. I can see now that he has the same reddish brown hair, cut to a spiky shortness, and I guess that he's Claire's brother. Jenna's uncle. "What did you say you did?"

"I'm a carpenter."

"That's helpful," Bill says. "We've got cops and the FBI and now a carpenter but nobody can find a goddamn clue about what happened."

"Where's Jenna's father?"

"Come and gone. He's really not part of the picture."

I can sense that Bill is angry, but not at me. Someone has taken Jenna, but there's nothing he can do about it. If he could, I'm sure he would find the guy who took her and beat him to death with a crowbar. But he's as helpless as anyone right now.

"Do you have anything of Jenna's that I can take a look at?"

Bill has been leaning against the countertop, arms folded across his chest. Now he pushes himself off and takes a step toward me. "Buddy, I don't know who you are, but we've dealt with enough freaks already."

I've had about enough of Bill and I meet him halfway across the kitchen. "Get me something of Jenna's and I can help find her," I say quietly. I can tell by the expressions on the faces in the kitchen that they are doubtful.

"You should be going now," Bill says, taking another step toward me. I'll walk you to the door."

"I had a little girl once," I say quietly. "Let me help you find yours."

I haven't wanted to use Emily like this because it doesn't seem right, but a child's death is like a talisman. Bill stares at me for the space of a heartbeat, then his eyes flicker away and he marches out of the kitchen. When he returns, he is holding a bright pink backpack. He thrusts it at me angrily. "I don't know what the hell you're up to, but I'm ready to throw you out on your ass."

I nod, taking the backpack from him. Right away I can tell I'm not going to get much from it. I close my eyes and try to concentrate. My breath goes out and I let my mind go blank. Maybe there are too many people watching. I close my eyes. Behind me, someone is whispering. Long minutes pass, but it's no use.

"Pink is Jenna's favorite color," her mother explains when I open my eyes.

"See what I mean," Bill says. "Another goddamn crackpot."

Nothing happens as I stare at the backpack in my hands, feeling disappointed. Still, I sense something there. Not ready to give up, I start unzipping the pockets. There are do-dads and key chains hanging off the zippers. Finally, deep inside the big central pouch, I find a spiral notebook. JENNA is written across the front in big, fat letters decorated with stars and miniature flowers. The notebook feels warm to the touch.

"She liked to write poetry," Claire says, her voice catching. "The police have already looked at it."

Holding the notebook in both hands, I close my eyes. All at once, I'm very far away. My mind drifts ... I see specks of dust dancing in the sunlight ... a tang of AXE aftershave in the air from some boy who has put on too much ... the bell rings, the halls are packed ... she says 'bye to some friends ... Madison says she'll come over later to do some homework ... outside it's still warm, almost summer ... she takes the shortcut down to Yellow-field....a small blue car passes her ... she has seen it before....the car pulls to the curb in front of her....nobody gets out and for the first time, a flicker of unease....use your head, her mother always says....she's being silly....she recognizes the Honda symbol on the trunk...a man gets out as she goes past....older guy, not a kid....she tries not to look at him ... just ignore him....that's when the hands grab her ... she tries to scream ... no God no this can't be happening ...

I come up for air, gasping like someone who has been under water for a very long time. I suck in another lungful of air. It was drowning that did it. They should have left me there under the water for another minute. My heart is pounding. Everyone in the room stares at me and I realize I've been talking, telling them Jenna's thoughts.

Bill comes up and takes the notebook out of my hands. I'm shaking so hard by now that he could knock me down with a finger. "I'm calling the police," he says in his gruff way. "A blue Honda. He snatched her in a goddamn blue Honda down on Yellowfield Boulevard. He was following her. Jesus Christ."

Someone helps me to a chair.

Jenna's mother sits across from me. She reaches out to take my hand. The expression on her face, bleak as a field of wheat stubble when I walked in, has changed. She looks at me with something like hope.

"How do you know?" she asks quietly. "How can you do that?"

All I can do is shake my head. Somebody brings me a glass of water. My hands shake so much that I can barely lift the glass.

One of the women, a neighbor I guess, reaches out and helps me bring it to my lips. The kindness of strangers. If only they knew the truth about me, they might not be so eager to have me in their kitchen.

"Who are you?" Jenna's mother asks.

"I'm nobody," I manage to say, my mind still spinning like a carnival ride. "I shouldn't even be alive."

The police have similar questions about who I am and how I know these things, but I give them a couple of names to call and detectives that I've worked with before vouch for me. According to the Connecticut State Police, there are at least ten thousand Honda sedans registered in the state. The records don't indicate how many of these cars are blue, but they can try to narrow the list to cars registered to men. The more helpful detail is that the abduction took place on Yellowfield Boulevard. The section Jenna would have walked on her way home from school is a residential area about three blocks long. Cadets from the State Police Academy volunteer to go door to door and troopers stop every car turning down the street, hoping that someone might have seen something if the drivers passed that way previously. The police are skeptical about me— but everyone is so desperate for some break in the case that they are willing to try.

Finally, the police stop a car driven by a teenager who lives in the neighborhood where Jenna disappeared. He confirms that he saw some guy and a girl in a car. Something didn't look right, but he just figured they were having an argument or whatever. Besides, he was just driving past. The guy at the wheel had a beard. And it was a new Honda Accord. The kid noticed, because teenage boys know cars. It's the first real break in the case.

I check into a Motel 6 on the highway and then head out again to staple fliers to utility poles. Jenna's disappearance is all over the news, so the convenience stores where I stop are more than willing to put fliers on the counter. The manager at an Exxon gas station takes a handful and helps me tape them to all the pumps outside. "You never know," he says. He gives me a cup of coffee and a free tank of gas, and then promises to fax a flier to every Exxon in New England.

For the next couple of days there's not much to do. I stop by Jenna's house a few times to sit with the neighbors and drink coffee in the kitchen. That's where I am when Bill comes chugging in under a full head of steam.

"Get up!"

"What?"

"Get up, you lying son of a bitch!"

As soon as I start to stand, Bill takes a swing at me. My arm blocks the worst of it but his fist scuds along my temple, catching me painfully in the ear. The chair crashes to the floor. He throws another punch but this time I knock it aside with a forearm that's tough as oak from six months of swinging a framing hammer and wielding a nail gun.

"Stop it!" Claire shouts.

A couple of men move to grab Bill. He shakes them off and jabs a thick finger at me. "You come in here to help us find Jenna, only you never told us you were a goddamn jailbird." The neighbors are staring at me. "That's right. He killed his own daughter. Got drunk one night and went for a boat ride, ran right into a barge. His daughter died along with a couple friends in the boat with them."

Claire asks, "Is that true? You killed your own daughter?"

When I nod, she turns back to the sink and continues rinsing out coffee mugs, slamming one down on the counter so hard that it shatters. I push past Bill and go out into the dark to clear my head.

————

It has been a long time since I thought of that night. Some things are better left alone, after all. You put them in a room somewhere in your mind and close the door, lock it if you can.

For a while, when I was in prison for manslaughter, I left that door open. I went over that one night again and again to the point where the edges of past and present began to blur, like I was caught in some video on instant replay. I realized that if I didn't stop, there was a chance I might never come back from that night. But now, it all comes back.

It's July. Hot and humid on the Chesapeake Bay as night comes on. I'm at the wheel of a speedboat that will go fifty miles per hour with the throttle wide open, which it is, showing off for a couple of old friends. Emily is laughing, wind streaming through her hair. She loves being on the water, which is why I bought the boat, using some of the insurance money left after my wife's death. Maybe it was a foolish way to spend the money, but it seemed like a way to find a little joy at a time when we needed it so badly. The drinking helped too.

The tug up ahead has two lights showing from the conning tower—or so I think—which means it's pushing a barge. Somehow, I've got it confused and as I point the bow to come around behind the tug there's a barge behind it. It's too late to change course and I think we'll be OK, but I can't see the tow cable in the twilight. The steel cable slices the hull in half lengthwise, like ripping the husk off an ear of corn, and we go straight to the bottom.

The water at this point is fifty feet deep, dark and full of currents. I'm not wearing a life jacket, and neither were my friends. But Emily had one on, and even as I go down I'm thinking she'll be fine, that the lift jacket will save her. She's a good swimmer. The thought calms me even as I grope around, trying to see in the murky water. There's no sign of the boat, no sign of Emily, no sign of anyone. The last of my air goes out in a long stream of bubbles and somehow I start to follow them. But I'm a long way down. The bubbles stop flowing out of me. I black out before I get to the surface. Later, I learn that the crew on board the tug fished me out just in time.

Later on, lying awake in a minimum-security prison facility

with that door in my mind finally closed, I opened another door and discovered the ability to reach out. They say that children are often the ones who are psychic, but as adults we forget or deny the gift. Trauma can bring it forth greater than before. Having been drowned and resurrected may have something to do with it. Then again, in the history of the world, I don't think there's been anything so cruel as that barge crew's good deed in saving me.

WHEN I SHOW up again a couple of nights later, it's Claire who answers the door. She hesitates, then steps aside to let me in. "There's some news," she says. "The police think they might have a lead. Thanks to you."

It's something about the blue Honda and a guy with a beard —and I stay late to see what happens. One of the police detectives comes by even though he's off duty. It turns out to be nothing by the time the Eleven O'clock News rolls around. While everyone is watching the TV, I go into the kitchen and pour another cup of coffee. Most of the lights are off except for a bulb above the stove.

Emily is at the kitchen table, eating a bowl of cereal. I lean against the counter and watch her for a long time. Brown hair and brown eyes that she got from her mother. She reads the back of the cereal box, crunching and slurping.

There's a sound behind me and I turn to find Claire staring at the table. I don't know how long she has been standing there, empty coffee cup in hand, but from the way she's staring at the table I know she's been watching Emily too. When I look at the table again, Emily is gone. There's not a bowl or a cereal box, just empty space. Claire is looking at me, white as a ghost herself.

"Will you show me Jenna's room?" I ask.

It takes her a while to answer. "Yes," she finally says, her voice creaking like a rusty hinge.

Of course, the police have gone through Jenna's room carefully, looking for any clues to her disappearance: any notes or anything that might have been a gift from the stranger who took her. But their search turned up nothing. Since then, Claire has put her daughter's room back in order. The bed is neatly made, covered by a purple bedspread decorated with big pink flowers. The two windows have pink curtains, drawn back so that the black glass reflects us as we move through the room. Maybe it's the mirror effect, but both of our faces look flat, one-dimensional....old and tired. Posters decorate the walls and I recognize the name of a boy band that Emily used to like. All across America, I realize there must be a million bedrooms that look pretty much the same as this one, give or take a few different posters and varying shades of pink.

"Did Jenna collect anything?" I ask.

"She loved her stuffed animals," Claire replies, nodding at a menagerie of animals gathered on the bed. "But I don't know that you could really call that a collection."

"Did she have a favorite?"

Claire considers for a moment, then plucks a tattered plush turtle from the crowd. The corners of her mouth curl up, and I realize it's the first time I've seen her smile. Claire's face, so ancient a moment ago, seems transformed. "Mr. Shell-shell," she says. "Jenna got him when she was three and for the longest time she wouldn't go to sleep without him."

I turn as Bill comes into the room behind us, the detective trailing after him. Bill is still angry at me for not revealing my past, but he sees Claire holding the stuffed animal, the hint of a smile on her lips, and bites back whatever it was he was going to say to me. "Mr. Shell-shell," he says, smiling himself. "Remember how one time Jenna left him at mom's and you had to turn around and drive back two hours to get him?"

Claire hugs the doll but her smile fades. "I hate this. Talking about Jenna like she's dead."

"She's not dead," I say. Bills eyes are hard as marbles as he looks at me. I ignore him and reach for the stuffed animal. "May I see that?"

Bill moves toward me. The cop in the door takes a step into the room, looking anxious. "Don't give it to him, Claire. He's going to pull that psychic crap again," Bill says, then glances at his sister. "He's just getting everyone's hopes up."

Claire hushes him. She doesn't say so, but I know she's thinking of what she saw in the kitchen. Claire hugs the turtle, crushing it to her, then slowly hands it over. My hands flinch away at first. The worn green plush feels like it came out of an oven.

"What's wrong?"

"I'm not sure."

I sit down on the bed, holding the burning toy. I close my eyes.

The rush, when it comes, is like riding a roller coaster in the dark. I drop into nothing, feeling the breath go out of me and the wind in my face. I am afraid. The walls disappear and I am surrounded by night ... floating high above the town, lights winking in the shimmer of summer heat ... there ... the house is a rancher a block down the street from a yellow Subway sign ... circling in closer ... all the way down to the basement ... at least, it must be the basement, so damp and cold, cinderblock walls ... fingertips bloody from scraping helplessly at them ... no light but a naked bulb in the middle of the room ... it's on all the time and there's a video camera up high above the locked door ... can't reach it because my ankles and wrists are bound with plastic ties....a smelly bucket in the corner ... he's coming ... brings me food on a tray but I can't eat, can't stand to look at him ... please ... where am I ... floating up again like following the bubbles from my lungs ... up through the rooms, the roof ... my vision narrows until it's like looking out a peephole ... he's not breathing, Jesus, I think his heart stopped ... better call 911 ... the detective is shaking me but I won't come back yet ... I see the numbers beside the front door in a pinpoint of light.

"Four-two-eight-four," I whisper. "You need to find the house at four-two-eight-four. A white Cape Cod."

Then I surface, sucking in air like a man drowning all over again.

THE POLICE WORK all night and find four houses in a fifty-mile radius with that address. Only one is a white Cape Cod and it also has a blue Honda in the driveway. In the first gray light of morning, the police burst through the door of the kidnapper's house. He is shot to death when he comes at them with a kitchen knife. They find Jenna in the basement and set her free. By that afternoon, she is home in her mother's arms.

WHAT FEW THINGS I own are already in the truck and I head out, back to Delaware. I know I'll get my old job back because guys walk off the job all the time, then walk back on when the bills start to pile up.

I only stop once for gas and coffee until I reach Delaware and I keep going into Maryland, where I get off the interstate and start down the side roads until I come to the Chesapeake. The water is calm as a bathtub and the beach is deserted except for Emily, who is splashing up to her knees. I call to her but Emily only wades in deeper, laughing. Soon I'm up to my own knees, then my chest. Emily swims ahead, going faster and faster, not waiting for me to catch up. A cold swell covers my head, bringing me to my senses like a slap in the face.

The spell is broken and when I come up for air, I'm up to my neck in the bay. One more step, maybe two, and I can let the water cover me for good. I wait for some sign, but Emily isn't out there. There's nothing waiting for me but darkness and the cold depths of the Chesapeake. I'm not ready to go just yet and I realize that just maybe, I can do more good between now and then. Slowly, I turn back and swim for shore.

CREAM SODA

Rob hadn't planned on killing anyone today, but there John had been, drinking the last ice-cold cream soda, sun beating down, and laughing at Rob digging around in the empty cooler in the middle of the campsite. Rob reached outside the cooler for one of the smooth beach rocks, palmed it, and in one smooth motion hit John while he was still swigging that soda. Did it make a sound? Hard to say, because all Rob could hear was the pounding in his head from John bragging all night and all morning about how well the store was doing. Never mind that he'd put Rob's father out of business selling things so cheap. The bottle of cream soda hadn't spilled, so he plucked it from John's dead hand and drained it in one long swallow.

ROAD TRIP

Not till we are completely lost or turned around ... do we begin to find ourselves.

    HENRY DAVID THOREAU, WALDEN or LIFE IN THE WOODS, 1854

He stopped at the Target to get a fresh white dress shirt for the funeral and to pick up some groceries. He was out of luck with the dress shirt, because all they had was "slim fit," which didn't work on his middle-aged body no matter how many miles he jogged. He would just have to hunt through his closet for something he could wear to the viewing.

He moved on to the grocery aisles, his mind wandering to Walt Whitman and that Allen Ginsburg poem, but what he noticed was not the grocery boys but a young woman who was the daughter of a friend, who came up to him and announced that she had made assistant manager at the store. He was distracted by her hair, dyed the color of rusty water. He wished her luck.

As usual now he skipped the chips aisle, the soda aisle, the candy aisle, and bought yogurt, whole wheat bread, low-fat milk, and some fresh vegetables. He had arrived at that age where he read all the ingredients. Did the yogurt have Aspartame? How many grams of sugar in the cereal? What about the partially hydrogenated oils? Funerals made you anxious about life's fine print.

He reached for a package of grape tomatoes, grown in Mexico, red and yellow, bright as the innards of a piñata. Mexico? Were those things even safe to eat? All those outbreaks of E. coli you read about. He put them back and picked up a cucumber, squinted at the sticker. Product of Canada, which sounded reassuring.

After all, he had taken a road trip there one summer when he was nineteen, up through New York state and Michigan. He remembered Niagara Falls at two in the morning, just a roar in the dark and mist on his face. The drinking age in Canada was eighteen and the speed limit was in kilometers, which was a novelty. He and his buddies got lost along the way, trying to see road maps by the dashboard lights.

They lived on Coca Cola and pizza and pitchers of beer. When he wasn't driving he read Faulkner and Styron in the back seat, chewing on the sentences like they were beef jerky. That was his Southern fiction phase back when he had literary pretensions. Now he wrote grocery lists and read labels.

In a campground one night he met a girl who was listening to a Cars tape on a boom box. What was her name? He wasn't sure he had ever actually known her name, but she had smelled like bubblegum and wood smoke.

He wished sometimes they had kept going and driven to California, or maybe to Newfoundland. You're only nineteen once, my friend, he muttered to himself. The road trip you are planning is not long enough.

He sighed, then glanced at his watch, remembering that he still had to get to the viewing. Time waits for no man, especially not for your sixty-year-old neighbor who has a heart attack while mowing the lawn.

He wanted to go back to the rusty-haired girl, shake her, warn her that there was more to life than stocking shelves. But he doesn't want to frighten her. And he knows that some things you have to learn on your own, even if it's often too late once you figure them out. Inspired now, he reached again for the Mexican tomatoes, tempting fate in his own small way.

ORIGINALLY PUBLISHED IN *CAPSTONE* MAGAZINE, Summer 2016.

PIRATE MOON

They hadn't meant to fight. Dana sighed and shook her head to clear it not only of the margarita fumes, but also of the zingers she hadn't thought of hurling back in time. Why was it that she always thought of that snappy retort too late?

Maybe it was just as well. She hadn't meant to argue with Christopher, and those zingers would be like twisting the knife. Her husband really was a sweet and kind man. It was just that lately, they had been getting along about as well as vinegar fries and ice cream. The margaritas hadn't helped.

It had been Dana's idea to come down to Rehoboth Beach for a few days of surf, sand, and sun. Just the two of them and some time to rejuvenate and reconnect. She wanted to be reminded of their single and carefree beach house days. If you couldn't be free and easy at the beach, then where could you be? But their workaday lives had trailed them like Peter Pan's shadow until here it was, near midnight, with Dana walking alone on the beach to clear her head and calm her spirit after yet another row with her husband.

This was one of their first trips to the beach without the kids, who were off having their own adventures at the age Dana and Christopher had been when they first met. Their daughter,

Lindsey, was away for a summer program at Tulane. Their son, Evan, was in France for the month.

It was different without the kids, and they were still adjusting to the empty nest concept. Still, she and Christopher had everything to celebrate and look forward to. And yet, there seemed to be an endless parade of bills for tuition and airplane tickets and car insurance. Not to mention aging parents who seemed more forgetful and who needed rides to medical appointments. It was a middle-age perfect storm.

In the end, so much of the tension came down to money, money, money. That was why, once again, they had been fighting tonight.

Stop, she commanded herself. *Practice some mindfulness.* She had just been reading a book about that. Well, not a book exactly, but an article in a magazine in the waiting room at her mother's physical therapist.

Dana took a deep breath. The lights of the boardwalk faded away. She passed a few couples and surf fishermen, but walked on until she was blissfully alone on the beach.

The summer night was clear and blessedly low in humidity. Moonlight sparkled off the sea so brightly that she could almost read a paperback novel. There was a full moon. Back home, hunters called it the Buck Moon, but here at the beach it was known as the Pirate Moon. The story was that the buccaneers who once prowled the Delaware Coast would come ashore and bury their treasure by the light of this summer moon.

Beach scents reached her: salt air and seaweed, the fecund smell of the wet sand under her toes.

A tidal pool stretched ahead, no more than a few inches deep. As she stepped into the water, the pool felt invitingly warm from the residual heat of the day. Moonlight had turned the surface of the pool to liquid silver. Some trick of the light playing across the pool projected a shimmering prism of refracted moonbeams, almost like a doorway. Delighted, Dana spread her arms and walked through it. The ocean air on the

other side felt colder, but it must only be some trick of her imagination.

Walking on, she heard the skiff before she saw it. She heard
the knock of oars in oarlocks and the cadence of deep, male
voices. Peering toward the sea, she saw the dark boat
approaching shore, riding the gentle waves. Foaming surf seemed
to glow around the bow in the moonlight.

Dana thought that she must have come across more fishermen. She had heard that the fishing was good at night for sharks
and bluefish. Personally, she preferred a nice plate of coconut
shrimp.

She stopped to watch the boat come ashore. It was a wooden
dory about fifteen feet long, crammed with six men. They
jumped out and dragged the boat out of reach of the tide. So far,
they hadn't noticed her standing there against the dark backdrop
of the sand dunes.

Some of the men seemed to be carrying shovels. Not a
fishing rod in sight. Now she was curious. What were the men
up to? The men lifted what appeared to be a large cooler out of
the boat and struggled with it up the beach. The thing must be
loaded with fish, she thought, or maybe with beer.

As they came closer, she could make out details of what they
wore. Some had bandanas tied over their hair like bikers, while a
couple of others had large, wide-brimmed hats. Their shirts
looked puffy and loose fitting. She caught the glitter of a few
earrings. They looked like...pirates. Straight out of a Howard
Pyle illustration.

This was hilarious. She had come across a boatload of pirate
re-enactors! Considering the late hour, maybe they were getting
an early start on the next day by setting up their pirate camp
while the beach was empty. Her anger forgotten, she realized
that she couldn't wait to get home and tell Christopher about
this.

The man in the lead came close enough to spot her. Taken by

surprise, he halted abruptly and raised a hand to signal to the others to stop.

With his right hand, he reached for his waist and, to Dana's amazement, drew a sword from his belt. The metal made slithering sounds as it came free of the scabbard, just like in the movies.

"Who be there?" he demanded.

Dana decided to play along. "Just a lone damsel in distress, kind pirate sir."

The man advanced, keeping the cutlass pointed at her. She noticed that the other men now had blades drawn. She caught sight of a pistol or two. Some of her amusement faded. These weapons looked all too realistic.

"I can see the state of your clothes," he said. "Were ye shipwrecked or marooned?"

Dana wore shorts and a T-shirt, which was definitely underdressed compared to these men, some of whom wore heavy, wool coats with brass buttons that winked in the summer night. "More like cast out," she said.

"Do ye be a witch?" The captain punctuated the question with his sword blade.

Dana stifled a laugh. "Some might say that, but I'm not actually a witch."

The men advanced. Closer now, they really did resemble pirates. They were very convincing re-enactors.

One of the other men spoke up. "Captain Kidd, if ye don't mind me sayin', witch or not, she might have her uses on a night such as this."

"Aye," the man called Kidd said.

Kidd? Dana had spent the afternoon at the beach dipping into a book called *Delmarva Legends & Lore* and had read a chapter about pirate legends at Rehoboth and vicinity. Kidd had figured prominently.

She studied him more closely in the bright moonlight. He was well over six feet tall, and lean in the same way that a chunk of driftwood looks after being scoured by saltwater to the bare essentials, with a nose sharp as a blade and a pale scar down one cheek. The rest of his face looked tan to the point of being leathery. Fierce, dark eyes stared back at her.

Looking into that fathomless gaze, Dana actually felt chilled. She shook her head to clear it. "Must be the margaritas," she said.

The men crouched and swept their weapons in all directions. "Margaritas? Be they Spaniards about?"

"No, just some frozen blender drinks that go down too easy and are loaded with calories."

"She speaks in riddles," said one of the pirates. "How do ye ken that she's not a witch?"

"Witch or not, she'll do for tonight." Kidd waved his sword. "Look lively and grab her, lads!"

Dana turned to run, but before she could move, two of the pirates grabbed her arms. They were not big men—no taller or heavier than she was—but they were inordinately strong. She still tried to run, but they lifted her so that her feet seemed to be on an imaginary treadmill. The pirates laughed heartily at the sight. Up close, they smelled like alcohol, tobacco, and a lack of bodily hygiene. There was something almost other-worldly about these men, as if they had rowed that skiff out of time itself.

She thought about the prism of moonlight she had stepped through. What if—no, it wasn't possible. But here were these pirates. And here was she.

They carried her up the beach and into the dunes. By now, Dana was terrified. Her heart pounded.

The men with the shovels set to work, digging. She looked more closely at the cooler. She saw that it was not a cooler at all, but a wooden chest.

"A treasure chest?" she wondered aloud.

Kidd barked a laugh. "Aye, a treasure chest. Brought ashore for safekeeping. The damned Royal Navy wants to hang me from a yardarm, so we need to leave these waters for a spell. Dig it deep, boys!"

Another pirate spoke up. "Shall we still draw straws, Captain?"

"Scupper that! No need for straws when we have a God-given sacrifice this night. What better curse than the blood of a damsel?"

Dana did not like the sound of that. "Excuse me?"

Kidd explained. "A treasure chest needs a curse to protect it, ye see. Normally, the lads here draw straws to see whose blood will be spilled so that his spirit will guard the treasure and curse any who might try to steal it. His bones are buried with the treasure. But tonight, we have you!"

Dana tried to get away. The men had iron grips. They simply laughed harder when she struggled. Down in the hole, two pirates dug deeper into the sand.

"Let's have a drink while we wait, lads," Kidd said. From a deep pocket of his coat, Kidd produced a bottle of liquor.

The liquor made its rounds. They offered her the bottle, but she refused with an emphatic shake of her head. This made the pirates laugh all over again.

Kidd walked over to the treasure chest and flipped open the lid. The pirates paused in their digging and drinking long enough to gather around and admire their plunder. Gold coins gleamed in the moonlight. Gemstones glittered.

With the pirates distracted, Dana saw her chance. She reached out and grabbed both pistols out of Kidd's belt. She jabbed the barrels into the men flanking her, forcing them to release her and step back.

"Over there with the others," she ordered. She now had all six pirates in front of her guns.

"Now, missy," Kidd began in a reasonable tone.

"Don't missy me, you freaking pirate!" Without letting go of the pistols, she used the heels of her hands to pull back the hammers on both guns to cock them.

Kidd's grin faded, and his voice took on a harder tone. "Two shots, missy—and six of us."

"Yeah, but there's gonna be just four of you when I get through. Who wants it first?"

She knew that Kidd had a point. These were pirates. Men experienced in brawling and bloodshed. She didn't have long. Maybe they didn't value their lives, but there was evidently one thing they did value.

"Steady now." The captain kept one hand on the hilt of his cutlass.

Dana stuck one pistol under her right arm. The pirates stepped closer. Then she reached into the chest, grabbed a handful of coins and gems, and flung them into the dunes.

The pirates gasped as one. She grabbed another handful of coins and hurled them away. "Step back!" she demanded.

The pirates obeyed. They glared at her with anger, even hunger. She had no doubt what would happen to her at their hands if she let go of the pistols. They had already promised to kill her. Now her death threatened to be painful and tortuous. She had no doubt that pirates might be endlessly inventive when it came to torture.

To buy herself time, she grabbed another handful of coins and gemstones. "Back!" They moved away, but she threw the coins anyhow. Kidd groaned as if in pain.

She knew the standoff couldn't last forever. It was now or never. She grabbed the pistol tucked under her arm so that she was double-fisted once again.

She pointed the pistol in her left hand and pulled the trigger. The pistol bucked like a thing alive, and the boom left her ears ringing. This was sure as hell no movie prop. This was a hand-held cannon.

At the gunshot, the pirates flinched and ducked, wondering who had been hit. Dana had pointed just above their heads, not quite able to bring herself to shoot anyone.

She dropped the empty pistol, scooped up another huge

handful of gold coins in her left hand, and ran. It wasn't much of a head start, but it was enough. A couple of shots rang out, but the pirates missed. She still had one loaded pistol and a handful of treasure.

She fled down the beach. Her only hope was to reach Rehoboth. But ahead, all she saw was empty moonlit beach. The distant lights of the boardwalk and beachfront hotels were nowhere to be seen.

Behind her, she could hear the pirates pounding down the beach after her, shouting curses and threats about what they were going to do to her. Having no interest in being drawn and quartered, she ran faster.

Dana was barefoot and fleet running across the sand, while the pirates wore heavy clothes and boots that weighed them down. Her occasional treadmill workouts and morning jogs gave her an advantage over men who spent most of their lives pacing the deck of a ship. However, one spry pirate was barefoot and outran the others. She could hear him just behind her. Unlike the other pirates, he didn't waste his breath shouting about what he was going to do to her. At any moment, he was going to catch her.

Dana spun, leveled the pistol, and fired. She flung the gun away and kept running, not bothering to see if she had hit him or not. The moonlit beach seemed to stretch ahead endlessly. If she tripped or stumbled in the damp sand, the pirates would be on her instantly.

And then she saw it. That same weird shimmer off the tidal pool. She splashed across the water and right through the prism it projected. Her feet disturbed the pool so that the light scattered in her wake.

Instantly, the air turned warmer. She saw the lights of Rehoboth ahead. They looked magical and welcoming on this summer night. She turned and glanced behind her and saw that the beach was empty. She kept running toward the lights of

Rehoboth, back to the crowds of twenty-first century people, back to her husband, Christopher.

When she returned to the rented beach house, she found him on the deck, waiting for her. The scene was so tranquil that she could scarcely believe that she had been running for her life just a few minutes ago.

"Dana, where have you been? I've been worried sick. You forgot your cell phone and I couldn't reach you." He paused. "Look, can we press the reset button on this trip? It's so stupid to fight over money, of all things. I'm sorry."

Breathless, she hugged him. He felt a little soft in the middle, and he wore a neon-green polo shirt rather than a wool coat. He smelled pleasantly of coconut-scented sunscreen. One thing for sure, he was no pirate.

Then she let go of him and dumped the big handful of coins and gems on the little deck table. Somehow, she had managed to hang on to them during her escape. The gold had value, of course, but she'd read somewhere that Spanish doubloons could be worth as much as a small beach house to the right coin collectors. Mixed among the coins were green and red gemstones. Who knew what those rubies and emeralds were worth? Christopher's eyes widened.

Perhaps it wasn't a fortune, but it was enough.

Dana smiled at the look on his face. She couldn't imagine that any sort of argument had driven her away from him, out into the moonlit night. Their quarrel seemed so foolish now, although it had taken a band of bloodthirsty pirates to make her realize what really mattered. She had Captain Kidd to thank for that—and for their newfound riches. "I'm sorry, too," she said. "And I'm pretty sure that we won't be arguing about money, not ever again."

ORIGINALLY PUBLISHED IN *BEACH FUN: Rehoboth Beach Reads*, 2018.

THE MIDNIGHT SERVICE

My name is Slats Hennessey and I just turned 19 years old. My real name is Matthew, but everybody calls me Slats because I used to be so tall and skinny. I'm six-foot-three and the joke in high school was that you could count my ribs right through my shirt. But two years of college and sitting around not playing basketball or baseball gave my body a chance to fill out, so that now you can't see my ribs anymore and I have a sort of potbelly when I slouch.

I'm thinking of my ribs, and how they used to stand out like the thin wires of a birdcage, because I'm home for Christmas. No sooner do I walk in the door than my mother gives me sugar cookies shaped like angels and stars, colored with sprinkles of green and red sugar. She's a great mother, short, wearing an apron, and when she hugs me she smells like baking and apples and perfume. She's always wanting to "put meat on my bones," she says. I know I'm home.

"You grew." She looks up at me and smiles. "You must be taller than your father by now."

"I don't know," I say, talking around a mouthful of cookies. "You look great, Mom."

I haven't grown, of course. I haven't gotten any taller since last year, just thicker. My father and I are exactly the same height.

So I sit down and my mother carves slices from a cooling ham to make me sandwiches on fresh-baked bread. She pours herself a cup of black coffee and sits down across from me with a single cookie while I tell her about school, final exams, my crazy roommate. At 5:30 we hear a car pull into the driveway and my mother jumps up to get the door. I sit at the table, sipping coffee, and I hear my father striding through the house on his long legs, yelling "Slats!" until he comes into the kitchen all grins and handshakes. The three of us fill the kitchen that smells like baking cookies and ham, smiling and laughing and not really hearing what anyone else is saying. My dad throws his briefcase and coat into the corner and we sit down to eat, the three of us together, talking and eating for hours until we begin to yawn and it's time for bed.

"LOOK at what your father brought me," my mother says, leading me through the house. On the dining room table there are flowers in a vase, an arrangement of reds and whites.

"That's nice," I say. "They're perfect for Christmas."

Dad is in the living room, reading the paper. The news is on TV. He's still wearing his tie, though it's loosened, and there's a bottle of beer on the table beside him, making a puddle on the coaster.

"I can't believe you still buy Mom flowers."

"Your mother's a wonderful woman," he says, looking up from the paper. "I like to show her I haven't forgotten."

"I think it's good, how you two get along."

I go into the kitchen, where Mom is mashing potatoes. The muscles at the back of her arm tremble. It's hard work, but she loves to cook, especially during the holidays. Sometimes in the summer, though, my mother decides it's too hot to cook and we go out to eat.

She's still dressed for work in her office clothes. I notice her earrings, tiny golden scallop shells. They make her look girlish and pretty even like this, working in the kitchen.

"Hey, you got new earrings," I say.

"Your father bought them."

MY PARENTS CELEBRATED their 25th wedding anniversary in July and had a ceremony to reaffirm their vows. I suppose if they hadn't been my parents, the ceremony would have been dull. The minister read in a sonorous voice, summer flies bumped against the screens, trying to get out, and it was so hot that the women in the pews fanned themselves with the songbooks. Seeing them side by side at the altar, and my tall father bending down to kiss my mother, I wanted them to be happy.

All through the summer he gave her things: stuffed animals, candy, a bracelet. Or else he just walked into the house at lunchtime, his shirtsleeves rolled up, with a bunch of flowers in his hand.

"You're wonderful," he told her.

THAT NIGHT AFTER DINNER, the telephone rings. My mother goes into the kitchen to answer it and comes back a moment later.

"They hung up," she says. "I guess it was a wrong number."

The TV is on, though nobody is watching it, and the sound is turned down low. My father is looking through the paper again and my mother has a novel she reads through the crescent-shaped glasses balanced on the end of her nose.

There's a fire in the fireplace, the Christmas special buzzes on TV, and the pages of Dad's newspaper crackle. I start to drowse off over a book I'm pretending to read.

Dad gets up and goes into the kitchen. I can just see his back as he picks up the phone and stretches the cord around the corner of the refrigerator, out of hearing. After a while he comes back in and settles down with another bottle of beer and the paper.

"I was just calling Jack from the office," he says after a minute. "I had to get some things straight for tomorrow."

Suddenly, my mother is crying. She takes off the glasses and wipes at her face with her fingers, as if trying to push the tears back into her eyes.

"What's wrong?" I ask, half-standing from my chair, alarmed.

"Nothing," she says, her voice choking as she tries to get control of herself. "Nothing at all. I'm just so.....happy." She sniffles. "Everything is just so happy.

Dad doesn't say anything. He just stares hard at his paper and takes a long drink of beer.

OTHER CARS STREAM into the church parking lot for the midnight service. All the windows of the church glow with yellow warmth and the pattern in the round, stained glass window above the heavy double doors shines with cool greens, reds and blues. An old man in a hat holds the church door open for his wife, flooding the broad stone steps with light. Someone inside grips his shoulder in greeting as he takes off his hat.

"You couldn't get me to go to church Christmas Day," Dad says, opening the car door. Cold air washes in and the overhead light comes on. "All those screaming kids so excited from opening presents."

"This is nice," says Mom, looking at the church. "It seems holy, Christmas-sy, like it should. Did you bring the collection envelope?"

"Yes," he says. "It's in the glove compartment."

She reaches for the knob.

"Don't bother, honey," Dad says. "I'll get it."

But she is already turning the catch. The compartment opens and a small, gift-wrapped box falls onto the ledge of the open door.

"Oh!" she says. She looks at Dad and smiles. "Were you going to surprise me?"

He grins back. "We have to save it for tomorrow."

"I don't want to wait," she says. "Let me open it now. It's Christmas Eve. You're allowed to open one present on Christmas Eve if you want."

She picks it up, her hand just ahead of his as he moves to take it away. His smile is gone and he watches her nervously, leaning toward her.

"It's really—" he starts to say, then pauses and tries again. "I bought it for one of the secretaries at work, you know. We give them little things at Christmas."

"I just want to see what it is," she says, smiling, as her nail delicately slits the tape and she unwraps the package without wrinkling the paper.

Inside the box are two gold earrings in the shape of scallop shells.

"You bought her the same thing," she says, speaking very softly. "How could you? I won't stand it anymore. I won't have you calling her at night." She's crying now. "'Jack from the office.' Do you really think I'm that stupid? Don't ruin everything."

She sobs, hunched down in the seat. The box has fallen onto the floor. Dad picks it up, the box, the wrapping paper, and the earrings like two bright eyes, and throws them out the door. In the darkness I hear the metal ring as it bounces on the cold asphalt. He shuts the door.

Mom stops crying and wipes her face, pats her hair into place. We get out of the car, silently, and walk toward the church, where the choir has already begun to sing so that a little of the music carries out to us. They hold each other and I walk slightly behind and to one side. We go up the steps and into the church, on Christmas Eve, a family.

ORIGINALLY PUBLISHED in *The Baltimore Sun Magazine*, December 23, 1990

THE FOX WENT OUT ON A CHILLY NIGHT

Chickens ran everywhere, spewing in terror across the yard. They cackled and ran on scaly yellow legs all around him. They flew into his face, tripped up his feet.

It was afternoon. The sun was hot. Jake ran toward the coop. He ran hard, with his boots thumping fast, pounding the cracked dirt. Hot air rasped down his throat and billowed papery lungs. The gun was heavy, with light shifting, gliding black, white, bright across the oily metal. The chickens cackled and flew around him.

The big red face of the fox glowered out of the coop door. Following it came a taut body, muscles curling across rust-colored flanks. The mouth opened on the head huge as a horse's and a glistening pink tongue lolled out between white-spiked fangs. The fox looked at him with its pale green eyes and snarled. The fox came closer. Jake saw the black silhouette of a man in the pupil.

Jake sat up in bed. Cool autumn air sluiced away his fear.

The night crackled with silence. A hint of starlight flowed through the wavy glass window, through the calico curtains. Blue starlight spilled onto the wood floor, rolled up the walls, danced in the old man's sunken eyes.

"What's the matter, dear?" asked his wife, beside him.

"Nothing," he answered.

"Did you have a bad dream?"

"No."

"Was it about the fox again?"

"Of course not."

"You shouldn't let that old fox bother you. He's been raiding the coop for the last ten years."

"But that was the fourth time this month."

"He's getting old. Chickens are much easier to catch than rabbits, I should think."

"Go back to sleep."

"Poor old fox."

He'd had enough of the fox wrecking his dreams. It was four o'clock and he could not sleep. Jake eased out from the covers, creaking as much as the bed.

He knew where to find the fox. He had seen him before, crossing the frost-silvered meadow beyond the woodlot, as dawn crept up the horizon.

Darkness still shrouded the sky, speckled in places with glittering stars. To the east the gray was congealing, preparing for a brilliant-hued autumn dawn.

Jake sat down in the long grass at the top of slope, where he had a good view of the meadow below. The silvery grass crackled beneath him.

Stroking the cool blue barrels of the shotgun, he remembered. He remembered getting the gun ten years ago, the first time that the fox had raided his coop. Other memories drifted through his mind. They seemed like fragments of another life. Moving to the country was a memory, moving after teaching English in the public schools of Baltimore for thirty years.

"It's so beautiful," said Penny as they pulled up in front of the white, two-story farmhouse.

Inside, the house smelled like apple pie and sausage.

On the table in the kitchen stood a jar of blackberry jam and a loaf of bread. "Welcome to our neighbors," read the little note tied around the jar with a piece of coarse brown string.

"We should have moved out here years ago," he murmured as he hugged Penny close.

The summer afternoon melted into mellow evening. After putting up hay, there was supper with cold spring water and frothy milk. They slipped away after supper to chase fireflies in the lingering July twilight. Swooping across the new-cut field, they filled a canning jar with fireflies. When the stars began to spark, they opened the jar, watching happily as the green lights blinked away and were gone.

Unbidden, even older memories came to him. He remembered going hunting as a boy with his uncle.

He'd seen movement in the brush on the edge of the woods. It was a deer. He raised his rifle.

"Steady, now," said his uncle. "Take your time."

The rifle smashed into his shoulder, crashed in his head. The spent shell turned end over end when he ejected it. The deer lay kicking, then dead in the honeysuckle. His eyes watered as he stared down at the brown body. That had been his first and last deer.

A flash of rust-colored fur brought him back to the present. Below, the fox separated himself from the brush and trotted across the meadow. His head and white-tipped tail hung low as he snuffled in the thick meadow grass.

The fox jerked his head up and caught sight of Jake. Their gazes met across the meadow for a few seconds and they seemed to come to some agreement; then the fox moved on, searching for mice in the dying grass. The old man didn't bother to raise the shotgun balanced across his knees.

Then he lay back on the slope and watched the run rise through the pink-purple clouds.

ORIGINALLY PUBLISHED IN *IMPACT* MAGAZINE, February 1985.

LAST STAND AT TURKEY POINT
LIGHT

T he day that the Coast Guard troops drove into Turkey
Point, Annie Poole stood out in the keeper's yard to greet
them, looking much like the lighthouse she stood beside. She
was tall and proud, but a little thick on the bottom, as one might
expect from a fifty-something widow.

Dubiously, she eyed the two trucks carrying Coast Guard
troops as they rolled into the yard beside her keeper's house.

The roar of the trucks caused Coolidge to rub anxiously at
her ankles. The peace of the high bluff overlooking the upper
Chesapeake Bay was broken.

"Government orders," Annie said to Coolidge, and sighed.
"There's a war on."

Now, here was the war at her door step. Once the trucks
stopped, the Coast Guard troops piled out. She hadn't known
quite what to expect, but not this. They looked like high school
boys, not hardened troops.

The one exception was a man who might have been old
enough to be their scoutmaster, or their father. He got out of a
truck and approached, walking a bit stiffly from the long ride
down the dirt road.

"Ma'am," he said, taking off his hat. She had seen newborn

babes with more hair on their heads. He introduced himself as Thomas Heyward. "We're under orders to guard the lighthouse and secure this station against any enemy incursions."

"It's a lot of government foolishness, if you ask me," Annie said.

Heyward stiffened at that comment. "This lighthouse needs protecting, ma'am. *You* need protecting."

"We'll see about that." Annie sniffed, sounding haughtier than she'd meant to. Tending the lighthouse on so many cold nights had left her with a permanently runny nose.

Heyward turned away without further comment and started shouting orders to the Coast Guard boys, leaving Annie feeling as if they'd gotten off on the wrong foot.

Just two days before, Annie had received word that her light-house—there was no way to think of it but as *hers*—had been deemed a strategic asset. One in need of military protection. She had been informed that a detachment of Coast Guardsmen would be sent to secure the lighthouse grounds for the duration of the war.

It all seemed more than a bit silly to Annie. The biggest threat she faced was the occasional fox or hawk that wanted to carry off one of her chickens. Now, the United States government was concerned that German U-boats might come up Chesapeake Bay to capture her lighthouse.

The situation would have made her late husband chuckle. As a lifelong lightkeeper, he had been well-used to the government's approach to management. He used to say, "Annie, rest assured that most government officials would rather shoot mosquitoes and swat elephants."

Annie was well aware that she had been the beneficiary of the government paying attention to details at times. It was President Coolidge who had signed a presidential order appointing her lightkeeper, overriding any objections about appointing a woman to the post. She had named her tomcat in his honor.

She also had to admit that the government had a point in

claiming that Turkey Point Light was strategically important, located at the entrance to the Chesapeake & Delaware Canal. With the war, the canal had been particularly busy with ships carrying freight and personnel for the war effort. As part of the intracoastal waterway, the canal provided a route between the ports of Philadelphia, Baltimore, and Norfolk without having to enter the Atlantic, where U-boats did prowl. At night, people lined the beaches of Atlantic City and Cape May to gape in horror at the glow of burning ships far out at sea.

Annie watched the ships and tugs pass below, bound for distant ports or even for Europe, while she herself rarely left the lighthouse grounds.

Annie had become so self-sufficient that she almost took it for granted that there was a world beyond Turkey Point. Her world revolved around the 35-foot tall brick lighthouse built in 1833 by John Donahoo on a 100-foot bluff overlooking Chesapeake Bay. There were few spots so beautiful—or so remote. All the materials for the lighthouse and keeper's house had been brought in by boat.

The lighthouse was located at the end of a peninsula, and it was twelve miles up a dirt road through the woods to the town of North East. With the nearest telephone and store that far away, Annie grew most of her own food, keeping a garden and chickens. She caught rockfish whenever she wanted. A generator now provided electricity to operate the fog bell, but for more than a century the lightkeepers had been expected to ring it by hand throughout the night, which was an exhausting task.

Trying to ignore this new intrusion by the outside world to her secluded duty station, Annie went about her chores as usual, feeding the chickens, tending the vegetable patch, and lighting the lamp, of course. Meanwhile, the Coast Guard set up wall tents in the field near the lighthouse. They established what they called a "listening post" on the cliff. Sentries were posted and watches established.

The young Coast Guardsmen had a few single-shot Springfield carbines, left over from the Great War, that they had to share when on watch. She put more faith in the old double-barreled Iver Johnson shotgun she kept in the lighthouse to scare off the hawks and foxes. Annie was no military expert, but without so much as a machine gun or a mortar, she had to wonder just how much protection the Coasties were supposed to provide if German commandos stormed the beach.

The Coast Guard had its new listening post, but Annie had her own—a bench where she liked to sit on the bluff, looking toward the west. She and Mr. Poole sometimes went down there in the summer or fall, to have a mug of coffee after supper, and watch a brilliant Chesapeake Bay sunset.

This particular evening as she sat on the bench, there was no sunset to see, but only a fading of the daylight as the fog rolled in. What some might view as forlorn, Annie saw as a variation on a theme. She loved to watch the bay in all its seasons and moods.

On evenings like this, she missed Mr. Poole.

Mr. Poole had been several years older than Annie. In her mind, she still thought of him as *Mr. Poole*, although they had been equal partners as man and wife. On occasion, on nights that did not require one or both of them to tend the light or the bell, they made love in the creaky brass bed upstairs in the keeper's house, but it was a dutiful sort of lovemaking, each of them hoping to satisfy the needs of the other. They had found more satisfaction in a gentle companionship. They'd never had any children. Annie sometimes thought of the lighthouse itself as their child, because they had tended and loved it together, carrying out the countless chores from filling the lamp with oil to polishing the Fresnel lens to whitewashing the brick walls inside and out.

Mr. Poole had been a hard worker, busy from dawn to dusk and beyond, and he was also brave. She remembered how one night a vessel had foundered in a storm. She and Mr. Poole had made their way down the cliff path, lighting the way with a lantern, and peered out at the storm-tossed bay. The surface of the water, usually calm, roiled with whitecaps. They could hear the pitiful cries of men in the dark, but could not see the wreck.

Mr. Poole had taken a boat and rowed out. Annie was sure it was the last that she would ever see of him. But he had returned, ferrying a cargo of shivering survivors. Then he had turned the boat around and gone back for the rest of the crew. By some miracle, the little boat made it back with the remaining survivors before the wreck slipped beneath the waves.

The lighthouse service wanted to give Mr. Poole an award in front of Congress for saving those men, but he wanted no part of that. Instead, some official had driven the many dusty miles down to Turkey Point and presented the award to him. Mr. Poole chuckled that night as he put the framed certificate away in a drawer. "Just doing my job, Annie, and just doing what any decent man would do. Everyone can be brave when they need to be. There's no cause to give a man an award for that."

That was quite a speech, coming from the taciturn Mr. Poole. Annie agreed with what he'd said, but she was proud of him all the same. They had made love that night in the brass bed.

Mr. Poole had died too young, after catching a fever from being up all of a damp winter's night ringing the bell.

Sitting on the bench, she sipped her coffee and felt pleasantly alone, rather than lonely. The fog shifted in her direction, carrying the smell of salt and damp on the breeze.

What was that?

She thought that she heard a diesel engine in the growing dark, and then a shout or two in what did not sound like English. Annie leaned forward, straining her ears, but the fog and the slight breeze did not blow her way again.

Just before it was completely dark, Annie returned to the lighthouse and sought out Mr. Heyward to report what she had heard.

"I wouldn't worry about it," he said. "The boys at the listening post didn't report anything unusual."

"Maybe if they actually listened, instead of talking about baseball and girls, they might hear something."

"Mrs. Poole, are you telling me that you actually heard a U-boat out there?" Heyward could not quite hide his look of amusement.

"Well, I know that I heard something." She sniffed.

Heyward was a level-headed fellow, so he doubled the guard that night. He made the boys give him all their bullets, though, explaining that he didn't want them accidentally shooting any duck hunters or fishermen in the fog.

AT THE OUTSET, the boys might have been disappointed that they weren't guarding some pretty young damsel in distress. She had a tower, but she was long past being Rapunzel.

Stuck in this remote duty, they made the best of it.

The Coasties had been sent to protect the lighthouse, but Annie soon found that she was the one protecting them.

She cooked up big pots of crab soup and made cornbread in her iron skillet, taking it all over to the lighthouse, which became a kind of gathering spot. On sunny days, the boys lounged on the grass in the shadow of the tower. She mended, tended to hurts and illnesses, and gave advice on broken hearts, or how to write a letter to a girl back home.

"Tell her how the blue sky over the water reminds you of her eyes."

"She has brown eyes, Mrs. Poole. Like leaf mush."

"For heaven's sake, don't write that! Just tell her that she has beautiful eyes."

"You reckon that's enough?"

Annie thought back to her own relationship with Mr. Poole.

Sometimes the best compliment had been a simple one. "I reckon it is," she said.

She taught them the rudiments of tending the light, and of the lightkeeper's duties, though she wasn't about to relinquish any of them herself. She did have them carry up the heavy cans of kerosene to the top of the lighthouse, and showed them how to keep the lamp filled. She warned them away from the cliff's edges, which tended to crumble precipitously. She taught them how to ring the fog bell. The pendulum mechanism for the bell descended into a deep pit, so she dragged some boards across the open pit to keep any of the more careless young men from falling into it in the dark.

THE COASTIES HAD BEEN THERE for six weeks when Mr. Heyward announced that he was taking all the boys for a night on the town.

"The boys are getting a little restless," he explained. "They need to blow off some steam."

Annie sniffed again, this time with genuine disapproval. She knew that "blowing off steam" was a euphemism for drinking beer in one of the roadhouses way up in Elkton, where there were likely to be loose young women from the munitions plants in town. Barefoot hillbilly girls, she had heard it whispered, had been bused in from mountain hollers down south to make bombs and artillery shells. Annie wondered what else those hillbilly girls might not be wearing.

Then again, she wasn't so naive that she didn't realize a young man needed something more entertaining than keeping watch over miles of empty bay and tending her vegetable garden. She worried about her boys, all the same.

"What about the Germans?" Annie asked. It had become something of a joke between them, since that night she had heard a diesel motor in the fog. There had been no further incidents, and the idea that a U-boat was going to anchor off the cliff and storm Turkey Point lighthouse now seemed ludicrous.

"I think the Germans will leave us alone for one night," Heyward said with a wink. He then added more seriously, "Besides, the weather is supposed to be clear as a bell. If they ever do attack, it's going to be on a foggy night when the spotter planes can't fly."

"Be careful up there in Elkton," she said.

"Aye aye." Heyward grinned. He seemed to be looking forward to getting away from the lighthouse for the night as much as anyone.

None of the young men wanted to be left out of the adventure, so it was decided that they should all go, it being unlikely that the Germans would pick that particular night to attack.

That was fine with Annie. She was used to being alone. In fact, she preferred it. But watching the two trucks drive off with the Coast Guard boys, it was the first time in years that she had felt lonely.

"I suppose it's just you and me," she said to Coolidge.

The cat rubbed contentedly against her ankles.

To keep that lonely feeling at bay, Annie kept busy. She was never one for sloth, but she doubled her efforts, pulling weeds in the vegetable patch, feeding her chickens, then finally climbing the narrow stairs of the lighthouse to give the Fresnel lens one last polish.

She stood back to admire her work. The lens was, in fact, more like a bejeweled sculpture in glass than a working maritime navigational aid. Its multiple layers and facets amplified the light almost magically, so that the beam reached for miles across the upper Chesapeake Bay.

Satisfied that not a single smudge marred the surface, Annie lit the lamp.

Soon after darkness fell, a heavy fog rolled in. The change in the weather was unexpected, but that was the Chesapeake Bay for you.

She looked down at Coolidge. "We'll be needing the fog bell tonight," she said to the cat. He followed her down to the bell, where she flipped the switch to start it.

Just before midnight, she went outside with Coolidge to check on the light. It seemed to be operating normally. But the fog bell had fallen silent. The bell was automated, driven by an electric motor run by the generator, and sometimes it stuck for one reason or another. Annie walked down to the bell and pulled back the boards covering the pit into which descended the two weighted chains that served as pendulums for the bell. Sure enough, with her flashlight, she could see that the chains had become entangled. She struggled to work them free.

In the quiet, she became aware of the sound of a diesel engine. Then a splash. Distinctly, she heard the sound of oars. Her ears strained to hear more. Then came the noise of a boat grinding ashore at the foot of the cliffs. Until that moment, she had been curious. Now, she was concerned. At her feet, Coolidge looked out into the darkness and yowled.

Annie was not sure what to do. Coolidge followed her down to the listening post—the one used by the Coast Guard, because it stood near where the trail led down the cliff to the beach. Voices. Surely, it couldn't be Germans coming up the cliff. It had to be duck hunters lost in the fog, or the crew of a broken-down vessel. Staring into the fog, she strained to see and hear.

Now, she heard footsteps. Stealthy ones. Slowly, the figures of several burly men came into sight, darker silhouettes against the backdrop of fog. She realized too late that her own silhouette was visible against the fog. The man in the lead froze as he caught sight of her. He turned and shouted something to the others.

Annie had still held out hope that she was being silly. This was all going to end with a laugh and offering a pot of coffee to some stranded duck hunters.

But the man's voice froze her with fear. He was speaking German.

Annie was still processing that fact when the German crouched and began to move toward her.

Annie snatched up the cat, and ran.

She knew that she could never outrun the commandos, much less a bullet. Fortunately, they hadn't started shooting; perhaps they still hoped for an element of surprise and wanted to take her alive. She glanced over her shoulder and saw two Germans close on her heels. They were going to catch her at any moment. She was a middle-aged woman, after all, and they were fit young men.

Annie swerved toward the bell pit. She knew just where it was in the dark, and leaped right across. Hard on her heels, the two Germans never saw the pit yawning in front of them. They fell 20 feet, screaming in terror, until they landed on the counterweights at the end of the chain pendulums, causing the fog bell to gong wildly. Holding Coolidge tight, she ran for the lighthouse.

She wasn't sure how many more Germans were after her, but all that she could think to do was to reach the lighthouse. The light was like a beacon to her, the same way it had guided the way for so many others on a dark night. The Germans must have slowed to see if they could help the broken men in the bell pit, because she managed to reach the lighthouse just ahead of them.

Annie didn't even have time to slam the door, and definitely no time to grab her old Iver Johnson shotgun and load it. She put down Coolidge and snatched up the first thing her hands touched, which was the cast iron skillet that she had used that morning to make a batch of corn bread. She swung it at the commando who ducked his head through the doorway. The heavy skillet was made in Erie, Pennsylvania, by the Griswold company, and weighed exactly four pounds. Joe Louis couldn't have delivered a harder knockout.

Dropping the skillet, she ran for the narrow stairs, with Coolidge leading the way. She had been up and down the lighthouse countless times so that her feet were quicker on the tricky, winding steps than the two clumsy Germans who came after her. But Annie soon reached the top of the stairway, and there was nowhere else to go but up the ladder into the cupola of the lighthouse. Once there, she turned and looked down at the two angry soldiers scowling up at her. Coolidge seemed to sense the danger, and caterwauled again. One man muttered something in German with a disgusted tone, and then started up the ladder.

Clutching Coolidge in her arms, Annie could only watch helplessly as the German ascended. What happened next was quite unexpected. One moment, Coolidge was hunkered in the crook of her elbow, and in the next, the tomcat had launched himself into the face of the German commando, claws extended. Coolidge stuck there like a burr.

The man howled, let go of the ladder, and hovered for a moment, arms pin wheeling. Then he plunged down the ladder and most of the way to the first turn in the winding stair, hit hard, and rolled down out of sight with Coolidge still clinging to him.

The remaining German stared into the wake of tangled tomcat and man, then looked up the ladder directly at Annie. He grunted what sounded like a curse and reached for his waist, where there was a gun in a holster. Annie closed her eyes, feeling awful about Coolidge, and knowing that this was the end.

But when there was no gunshot, she opened her eyes and saw that the German had drawn a knife instead, and was coming up the ladder. He had the knife clamped between his teeth like a pirate. The wicked, gleaming blade reflected the light from the lamp. Perhaps he felt the pistol would be too quick for the likes of Annie.

Desperate now, Annie picked up a jug of kerosene oil, used for fueling the lamp, and poured it over the commando.

Upon realizing that he was covered in kerosene, the German swiped at his face and muttered, *"Scheisse!"*

Their eyes locked across the short distance separating them. The German's pupils were black with anger. But the look in

Annie's eyes caused the German to stop with just a few rungs of the ladder left to climb.

In her hand was a wooden matchstick. It did not seem like much of a weapon, compared to the commando's knife, but his eyes grew larger when she struck the match against the brick wall and it flared to life.

"That's for Coolidge," she said, and dropped the burning match down the hatch.

Fortunately for Annie, the saboteur's clothes did not explode. He caught fire more like a giant lamp wick. Even so, the flames were enough to send the man hustling down the stairway, screaming in panic. He ran outside and rolled on the dew-wet grass to snuff the flames.

What was left of the commando squad regrouped a hundred feet away. They had been trapped, battered with a skillet, clawed, and singed. It was time for a new plan of action.

Annie climbed down, having to clamber over the body of the German that Coolidge had attacked; he must have broken his neck in the fall. Coolidge was nowhere to be seen, and Annie felt a stab of grief. On the floor of the lighthouse lay the man she had hit with the skillet. Not only was he still not moving; he wasn't breathing, either. Fear must have given her more strength than she realized.

While the Germans deliberated what to do next, Annie took action and loaded her shotgun. She ran out after them, brandishing the double-barreled 12-gauge. She never would have admitted it later to anyone, being a little ashamed of the fact, but she screamed like a banshee, wailing the rebel yell as she charged. Her keening howl of outrage sounded frightening even to her own ears.

Her battle cry lit the fuse of panic. What was left of the commando group turned and ran for their boat on the beach below.

Annie didn't bother to chase them down the trail. She dashed to the cliff's edge, and a minute later the fog parted just enough for her to spot the dark shape of a launch making its way out into the bay.

The German commandos were out of range by then, but that didn't stop Annie from letting them have it with both barrels.

THAT NIGHT, with their vision clouded by the fog and beer, the Coast Guard boys opted to camp on the dark and narrow dirt road. They arrived in the morning, cold and hung over. The sight that greeted them made them wonder if they might still be drunk. Two bodies lay in a neat line where Annie had dragged them. Broken and bloody, the corpses may as well have had X's over their eyes to show how obviously deceased they were, just like how dead men were depicted in the Sunday funnies.

Annie wasn't sure if she was more relieved to see the Coast Guardsmen or Coolidge, who showed up at first light, none the worse for wear.

She did, however, feel conflicting emotions about the dead men; it was not in her nature to harm anyone, even a German saboteur. She decided that she had only been defending herself —and the lighthouse—from attack.

Mr. Heyward expressed his astonishment, and then drove back to make a report. The nearest telephone was miles away at a Methodist church rectory. He returned with orders to bury the bodies in an unmarked grave, which they did. Everyone was sworn to secrecy. Heyward explained that the whole incident was to be hushed up to prevent public panic. Publicizing the fact that there were U-boats prowling Chesapeake Bay wasn't going to inspire confidence in the war effort.

The Coast Guard did not receive any reinforcements, and Heyward's superiors did not send the machine gun that he requested. Annie recalled Mr. Poole's words of wisdom about shooting mosquitoes and swatting elephants. All they got to defend Turkey Point Light was a box of hand grenades, which on

the Fourth of July they had great fun hurling off the cliff.
Everyone agreed that it was the best fireworks show they had
seen in years.

To the boys' disappointment, they never did spot another U-
boat.

Annie didn't mind.

ORIGINALLY PUBLISHED in *Bay to Ocean 2018: Best Writing from the
Eastern Shore Writers Association*.

BULLET BABY

The story of how I was born has been told and retold so many times, wandering this way and that like thistle down blown by the wind, that people are always coming back to me for the truth of it. I tell them what happened and they usually go away disappointed—not with my version of the story, which is a good one—but with me, the bullet baby. I suppose they think there should be more to me, something special, after coming into the world in such a strange way.

My story begins with a skirmish fought near the tiny Maryland crossroads town of Hoods Mill. No one has ever heard of it, not as they've heard of Antietam, Bull Run, or the Wilderness. Nobody is even quite sure why the skirmish took place, although the area was swarming with troops that summer of 1863 as a prelude to Gettysburg. What I tell people is that a band of Confederates was visiting the Hoods Mill home of some local soldier's aunt known for her fried chicken and white potato pie. In that area, a lot of young men had gone over to the South, including my father, who had grown up nearby in Baltimore. Stuffed silly and loaded down with the leftovers, the Confederate boys had stumbled across an equal-sized handful of

Yankees. The startled soldiers started shooting at each other and the rest is my own history.

THAT'S when my father was shot. He had some bad luck that day. No simple bullet wound through the muscle of the arm for him. No grazed temple bound with a gallant bandage. Instead, imagine how embarrassing it must have been for my father to have one of his testicles shot off. And there must have been those first few moments of terrible fear—was it serious, was he going to die—before he looked down and saw, perhaps felt with his hand, the bloody damage. His fellow soldiers wrapped him up as best they could, and he limped on toward the disaster at Gettysburg.

My mother was more seriously wounded. She had been sewing in between reading Sir Walter Scott, both tedious things young girls were encouraged to do in those days. She sat by an open window in one of the handful of houses near the Hoods Mill crossroads when the shooting started. She was there to catch a breeze, she always said, although I think she only wanted a good look at the young soldiers going by and a seat on the front porch would have been considered indecent.

Mother never actually saw the fighting, she told me, just some soldiers running in confusion. She jumped up from her chair at the sound of gunfire and at that instant a stray bullet came through the open window and struck her in the abdomen.

She always said it was lucky that she had jumped up because the bullet would have hit her heart or lungs if she had still been sitting in the chair. Still, the wound looked fatal enough as she collapsed back onto the carpet, a bright red stain spreading across the front of her white dress. My grandmother ran in, screaming, and my mother's eyes rolled back in her head. She told the story comically years later, although there wasn't anything humorous about it at the time.

For five days her soul fluttered around her body like a moth to a flame. She finally pulled through and recovered—the wound was a clean one and the Minié ball went straight through without harming anything vital.

The bullet had crossed the room and left a hole in the parlor wall. That bullet hole enraged my grandmother. She considered it bad luck, as if the bullet were a solidification of evil Yankee spirits rather than a bit of flattened-out lead. She had a handyman take down most of the wall before he could dig the bullet out of the lathe, and then he put up new plaster and re-painted the wall. Who knows what my grandmother did with that mangled Minié ball? Maybe she buried it or threw it on the trash heap. It's too bad, because I've always wanted to have that catalyst.

WHEN STRANGE CHANGES began to take place in my mother's body not long after she was shot, the doctor's news that she was pregnant caused a few tongues in the vicinity to wag. My grand-mother tried to tell people it had something to do with the bullet. Mother was from a good family and a nice girl, so many people were willing to be sympathetic, if not quite convinced. In quieter days, the scandal would have ruined her young life. But these were times of war and news was coming back to town of the dead, the names of local boys on both sides among them. Thousands had died at Gettysburg—so many that the towns-people struggled to bury them all. People in Vicksburg would soon be eating rats, their mules and horses long since served up. The pregnancy of a seventeen-year-old girl was barely a topic of passing gossip.

That didn't mean her pregnancy wasn't quite a shock for my mother, who still had only a vague idea as to how something like that came about. She wondered about outhouse seats and kiss-ing, until my grandmother explained the whole business to her after the fact. These days it's hard to believe a young girl could be so naive, but she grew up in Old Maryland and in a good family.

THIS IS where the good doctor enters into the story. Life might have been very different for my wounded father and unwed mother if it hadn't been for Dr. T.G. Capers of Baltimore. He was a kind man, my parents told me, although I wasn't old enough to remember him because he died not long after the war. Although he had Confederate leanings, he had traveled to Antietam and later to Gettysburg to treat the wounded on both sides.

He was a friend of my father's family, and having gone to work in the Gettyburg field hospitals, it was Dr. Capers who found him and treated his wound in the aftermath of that battle. My father had been captured, which was a blessing, because it meant that he received proper medical treatment and then was sent to Fort Delaware to wait out the rest of the war. Nonetheless, his treatment must have been just as embarrassing as painful, not to mention that he suffered from a young man's natural fear that he had lost something so valuable before ever getting the chance to put it to use. Even if the plumbing still worked, it might never be as good as new.

Meanwhile, back in Hoods Mill, my mother was becoming obviously pregnant and she soon gave birth to me, an eight-pound baby and healthy except for a wound on my belly that wouldn't heal. The local doctor was called in to treat me, accompanied by Dr. Capers, who had come out of curiosity upon hearing rumors in the medical community about my mother's strange pregnancy. The story goes that the doctors probed my festering wound and removed a tiny bit of lead—a remnant of the Minié ball. Dr. Capers knew where and how my father had been wounded nearby and began to put two and two together.

His theory clinched, he rushed back to Baltimore to write my father with the news that he was a daddy. I have sometimes wondered if Dr. Capers was a better matchmaker than a physician, considering his unusual medical theories.

Then again, I was born exactly 287 days after the battle, which was just the right amount of time. Dr. Capers theorized the Minié ball that had carried off part of my father's manhood was the same one to strike my mother, and the spermatozoa upon it had impregnated her. A far-fetched story, to be sure, but that's what the good doctor wrote my father at the Fort Delaware prisoner of war camp, and he must have been convincing. Not long after the war, my father returned home to Baltimore and days later showed up on the front porch of my mother's house in Hoods Mill, hat in hand, asking if he could see the young lady.

Who knows why my father went? Maybe he was still worried about his damaged anatomy and decided that this was his only chance at fatherhood and marriage. My mother certainly had few prospects, being an unwed young girl with a boy child, and when my father proposed she quickly agreed.

I do remember that my parents liked to laugh and that they were easy with one another. They must have kept a sense of humor about it all once they got over their shyness, having been complete strangers when they married. My father discovered that despite his embarrassing wound, certain functions were in perfect working order, because more children soon followed. Although my father was on the losing side, he had no great stake in the outcome of the War Between the States, and besides that, Marylanders at that time were mostly Confederates at heart, busy putting up monuments to the Lost Cause. My parents settled into my grandmother's house at Hoods Mill and had my three brothers and sisters, although none of them ever looked so much like my father as I did.

ALL THIS HAPPENED fifty years ago and my parents have passed away, leaving me to puzzle over the holes in their story. Half a century is a long time, and if there was some higher purpose meant for me after my unusual coming about in the world, I would have run across it. The only tangible difference it made in my life is the small scar on my belly that the Minié ball left. And I'm something of a living local legend of the sort who leaves whispers in his wake. But by now I think that my conception itself was the end-all be-all of my life, my greatest moment.

Consequently, I know I am a disappointment to some of the people around here, turning out the way I have. The local folks like to tell the story of my miraculous birth but they are reluctant to point me out on the streets of nearby Sykesville, where I conduct my trade. Their bullet baby is just the balding editor of the town newspaper there, not a blind seer or some strange being with a third eye blasted into the center of his forehead.

Still, I'm left with a good story to tell when all the others have run out and everyone is staring into their glasses, or there's only the sound of crickets to dispel the quiet on the front porch. In the quiet, too, old-timers will sometimes repeat the story of how they could hear the sound of Gettysburg's distant guns that July afternoon of Pickett's Charge.

Even now, there are those who say it's all a likely story and my parents probably had a fling that afternoon of the skirmish when the young soldiers, boys really, came to visit. They say it despite the evidence proffered by Dr. Capers, and my only defense is that it doesn't matter, anyhow. Believe what you want. That summer afternoon came and went in another century. But in this dull countryside people are reluctant to forget the excitement of the war when there were skirmishes and troops passing through, although there is already another war being fought in Europe that is every bit as brutal and cruel.

I have often wondered if there is a young girl in some French village with a fate similar to my mother's and some boy on a nearby battlefield groping at himself with a bloody hand. I only wish that I could introduce them and share the story of my own immaculate conception, to reassure them that miracles do happen when you trust in fate.

ADAPTED from the story first published in *ESC!* magazine, Summer 1993

THE WHEATFIELD WAR

And, Gallant Parker! thus enshrined
Thy life, thy fall, thy fame shall be;
And early valour, glowing, find
A model in thy memory.
— Lord Byron, 1814

When British forces moved toward Washington in August of 1814, Captain Peter Parker, the commander of the ship *Menelaus*, was sent up the Chesapeake with orders to create a diversion. His troops burned several farms near Rock Hall. This is a fictional account—true to the facts—about the American resistance he encountered several miles west of Chestertown at Caulk's Field.

———

IT WAS late August and the air was cool and dense with humidity. On such a breathless night, sound wouldn't travel far and the movements of soldiers hiding along the road would be muffled by the heavy dew. At least the night was with the Americans.

Under cover of darkness, Lieutenant Colonel Philip Reed

knew he had a chance to surprise the British as they marched up the dirt road from the Chesapeake. He wanted to make a flank attack, then slip away. He looked down the road that led to the spot where they would land their barges. There was no telling how large the British force would be, but it would certainly outnumber his 170 militiamen. An attack might confuse the British and turn them back, because they would be unable to tell in the dark just how many men Reed had. With luck, the British would hear nothing but crickets until the first musket shot.

"Watch out for any sheep, now," joked one of the militiamen near Reed. "I hear they're dangerous."

A few men laughed nervously.

"Quiet," Reed hissed. "There's going to be a lot more than sheep to worry about tonight, I can tell you. Now take your positions."

Without a word, the men walked off to hide themselves along the road in the tall wheat of Caulk's Field.

The incident with the sheep had made the men nervous all day. The previous night, after marching out from Chestertown, the men had bivouacked in St. Paul's Church. It was stifling hot inside the church, but that was better than being covered with the dew, and the heat lightning that danced over the Bay had threatened rain. All the doors were left open to let in whatever air was stirring.

In the early hours of the morning, the church was suddenly filled with shouts. "It's an attack," someone screamed. "My God, we're attacked!"

Men scrambled in the dark to find their muskets. Reed and his lieutenants restored order just in time to prevent the troops from shooting at each other in the dark.

Just as quickly as terror had spread through the church, there was laughter. A flock of sheep, made nervous by the approaching storm, had wandered into the church through the open doors. They walked over the men sleeping on the floor, and the soldiers, awakened from their sleep, had mistaken the sheep for British troops.

Still, nobody slept soundly after that. Until then the militiamen had all been in good spirits. It was lazy, late summer weather, and marching off to fight the British had all the threat of a Sunday picnic. But the incident with the sheep, coming as it had in the night, set the men on edge.

PETER PARKER GOT up from the table, checked to make certain his pistols were loaded, then sat back down. He wanted to be especially prepared tonight because he felt uneasy for some reason. He looked down at the blank page, not quite sure what he should write his wife.

So far, Captain Sir Peter Parker knew he had been lucky. But his success in burning the farm called Skidmore near Rock Hall on August 20 and then Richard Frisby's farm on Fairless Creek just that day had made him somewhat over-confident. He had encountered no opposition from the Americans. In fact, they pleaded with his troops just as they had when the British burned Fredericktown and Georgetown on the Sassafras River in 1813. The Americans had shown little mettle.

His activities on the Eastern Shore were really just a diversion, he knew, while the British attempted to take Washington, D.C. But there was no reason why he couldn't further his career with an accomplished campaign on the Chesapeake. At age 28, he was a rising star in the Royal Navy.

Parker wanted a real victory by burning Chestertown, but he knew taking the town would not be as easy as burning a few unprotected farms. His scouts (one of whom was a slave captured just that morning at Frisby's farm) told him the Americans had assembled a militia to protect their port; the Americans were camped not far from the Bay, the scouts reported.

Parker planned to land his men and march on the Americans that night.

With his quill he carefully wrote "H.M.S. Menelaus, August 30th, 1814," at the top of the page. He hesitated, though, before beginning the letter. To share his foreboding with his wife might seem cowardly afterwards if it came to nothing. There was a knock on the door of his cabin.

"Come in," he growled.

"Sir, the men are ready."

"Good," said Parker, without looking up. He held the tip of the quill poised above the page. "What about the slave. Do you think he'll be of any use?"

"He knows the land, sir, and where the Americans are. I think we can trust him."

"How do they seem?"

The officer smiled. "They can't wait to meet the ladies of Chestertown, sir."

Parker nodded, returning the smile. If they routed the militia, there would be nothing to stop them from marching on to Chestertown that night. He waited until the door closed before he began to write.

My Darling Marianne:
I am just going on desperate service and entirely depend upon valor and example for its successful issue. If anything befalls me I have made a short of will. My country will be good to you and our adored children. God Almighty bless and protect you all. Adieu, most beloved Marianne, adieu!
Peter Parker

P.S. I am in high health and spirits.

UNDER THE COVER OF DARKNESS, Lt. Col. Reed knew he had a

chance to surprise the British as they marched up the dirt road from the Chesapeake.

Reed stood in the road, studying the small hillside above it with satisfaction. The tall wheat hid any sign that more than one hundred muskets were trained on the road in preparation for the ambush. An opaque haze covered the sky with gauze, hiding the stars, but Reed guessed it was almost midnight. Here and there the wheat swayed as men fidgeted with their guns or tried to get into a better position for firing.

"Be still up there," he called as loudly as he dared. "Get into position and lie quiet. And do not fire until I give the word."

Suddenly, musket fire rattled down the road. Reed turned to see the flashes in the darkness. He had sent a small advance party to meet the British on the road in order to give the greater part of his force time to take positions in the wheat field. Another volley ripped the night apart as the British returned fire. Reed scrambled to hide himself in the wheat near the edge of the road.

As planned, the advance party came running past the hidden line of militia just ahead of the British. In the excitement, the British had strung out along the road as they chased the Americans. Reed guessed there were nearly 300 men and they were spread farther apart than he wanted. He would have to watch his flanks to make sure the British didn't get around behind his men. He raised his pistol, taking aim on a tall soldier just a few feet away.

"Fire!" he shouted, and the pistol leapt in his hand.

With the first volley, the British line staggered sideways. Several men lay sprawled in the dusty road and some were screaming. The militia continued to fire at will. They reloaded in the dark, sending scattered shots into the British line.

The British troops were amazingly disciplined. Obeying the shouts of their officers, the troops reformed and fired toward the hillside. Acrid gun smoke burned Reed's nostrils. Only a handful of the Americans had ever seen combat; most of them were just shop owners and farmers who knew how to handle a gun. They held their ground despite the tongues of flame that leapt from the British muskets.

Reed stood up. "Make each shot count," he yelled. "Watch the flanks."

A musket ball whined past his ear. Reed turned and fired toward a muzzle flash.

The British tried to advance into the field but the militia's fire held them toward the road. Reed watched as the British regrouped and directed their fire toward the militia's left flank.

The soldiers began to advance, one step at a time, toward his militiamen on the hillside.

"Hold 'em back," Reed shouted. "Hold the flank."

Wheat stalks crackled around him as men swarmed through the field to meet the advancing British line. The militia's fire held steady and the British fell back across the road.

"Sir, we're low on ammunition," said the lieutenant crouching at Reed's elbow. "Some of the men have already run out."

Reed looked down the line. Indeed, the shooting had slowed. Each man had only brought along 20 rounds and most of that had been used up in the exchange. But it may have been enough. The British line had fallen back and they only fired occasional shots toward the wheat field. Reed could hear the balls clip the wheat. Still, the British may just have been regrouping. He knew the militia could not withstand another frontal attack.

"Fall back," he shouted hoarsely to the lieutenant.

There was a low stone wall farther back in the field, and his line would stand a better chance if it had some sort of fortification to strengthen its position.

Reed's men crept backward through the wheat field. Some stopped to shoot toward the road, but the British muskets were silent. Vaulting over the wall, Reed struggled to see the road past the field. If the British attacked it would come down to hand-to-hand combat. His small force would be overwhelmed, he knew. Reed reloaded his pistol, using the last of his powder. He drew his sword with his other hand and waited for the final assault to come.

ON THE OTHER side of the battlefield, Captain Parker felt something go wrong with his leg. It was as if it had been struck out from under him with an axe. He collapsed in the road. "I'm shot!" he yelled, trying to keep the terror from showing in his voice.

Two men dragged him behind the line, away from the firing. Parker could just see the dark streak his blood made in the dirt road. There wasn't any pain — he just suddenly felt very tired. He lay on his back looking up at the darkness.

With the first musket shot, Parker realized with horror that he had led his men right into the American trap. They had no choice but to fight. Hidden in the field, the Americans made no sort of target. His men could only fire in the direction of the muzzle flashes. The American line held steady despite two attacks, and Parker fell back, thinking the force must be greater than his scouts had told him.

"Is it bad?" asked one of his officers, crouching over him.

Parker was about to answer, but realized the question was directed at one of soldiers who had dragged him off the road.

"Clean through his artery." The soldier spat. Parker told himself he must remember to reprimand the man later. He did not seem to have the strength right now. "Best get him back to the ship."

The officer went off in the dark to give the orders. Parker smelled the dry dust kicked up by the soldiers' boots. The gunfire and shouting seemed far away. *Adieu, most beloved Marianne, adieu!* He studied the sky and waited as a deeper darkness descended like fog.

A few weeks later, British forces made a sea and shore attack on Baltimore but were unable to take Fort McHenry, the stronghold guarding the city's harbor. The war continued elsewhere, but fighting ended in Chesapeake Bay.

Parker never made it back to the ship. His men carried him into a farmhouse at Caulk's Field, where he died in one of the beds upstairs. Fourteen British soldiers were buried on the farm. The British force returned to the Menelaus with Parker's body and 27 wounded. Parker had not wanted to be buried in America so his body was returned to England, preserved in a barrel of rum during the voyage. His famous cousin, Lord Byron, would write an elegy for his funeral.

MORNING DAWNED on the Chesapeake misty and cool. But after the sun quickly burned away the dew, the late August heat spread across the fields like a flood. At daybreak, Reed ordered that the one American killed be buried. Preparations were made for carrying the three wounded back to Chestertown.

The dirt road leading toward Chesapeake Bay was empty, marked only with boot prints and a few dark stains. Reed surveyed the field. Most of Caulk's wheat lay trampled on the ground and the crop was ruined. A small price to pay, he thought, for what had been won. He watched the men sitting a little apart, quietly eating a breakfast of cold biscuits.

"They're good men," Reed said to his lieutenant. "They're brave men." He looked west toward the Chesapeake where the British had disappeared. Then he walked off to find some breakfast.

ORIGINALLY PUBLISHED in *Chesapeake Bay Magazine*, October 1991.

COLE'S SOJOURN

Lucas Cole kept looking over his shoulder, expecting to see riders coming after them. If the Home Guard caught them, he and the man plodding along next to him would be hanged as deserters.

The Home Guard, made up of bitter wounded veterans or men who had found some way to avoid the fighting, patrolled these country roads constantly. What they wouldn't know was that Cole and Uriah Snodgrass were not running from the army but could be considered spies and assassins. They'd be dead all the same if the riders caught them.

When he wasn't watching out for the Home Guard riders, Cole glanced down at the road, trying to avoid the worst of the mud that threatened to suck the stolen Yankee shoes right off his feet.

Winter was a hard time to travel. Summer's dust had given way to mud, a cold slop that resembled congealed gravy. The mud liked to grab hold of feet and not let go. When the temperature plunged below freezing before dawn or after sunset, the mud froze and made the road easier, but the cold exacted its own price.

"Why are you so jumpy?" Snodgrass asked, noticing how

Cole kept looking around. Snodgrass tugged a ragged scarf more tightly around his neck. "There ain't nobody out here but us two fools."

"There's always somebody on the road."

"Listen now, if we do come across anyone, better let me do the talking," Snodgrass said. "You'll just shoot 'em."

"You try talkin'," Cole said. "And if that don't work, then I'll shoot 'em."

"Fair enough," Snodgrass agreed.

Cole carried a Sharps rifle with a telescopic sight slung over his shoulder and two pistols on his belt. In the Confederate army, Cole had such a reputation as a sharpshooter that none other than General A.P. Hill had decided that he would make a good assassin and had sent him to Washington City to shoot Union General Ulysses S. Grant. In Washington, Grant had narrowly escaped a bullet from Cole's Sharps rifle, so now Cole was headed to Grant's headquarters at City Point in Virginia to finish the business.

They walked on. Wind numbed Cole's face until his cheeks felt stiff as saddle leather. January's icy tongue flicked down his collar and wormed between every loose stitch. Cole did not remark on the cold. In fact, he didn't say much at all as they walked South. Snodgrass did plenty of talking for them both. Snodgrass had spent an hour that morning yammering on about summer and the sultry, languid air that a riverboat man got used to breathing.

Snodgrass was plenty vocal about the cold—complaining seemed to keep him warm—but Cole walked along as brooding and silent as ever, his eyes roving the winter landscape.

Snodgrass walked faster, seeming to know that the sooner they got off the road, the better. Whatever made someone like Cole jumpy made Snodgrass downright anxious.

They had decided to travel by day rather than scurrying along at night like a couple of blind possums. Besides that, the new moon meant that the night was black as an outhouse hole.

The frozen, rutted ground made travel slow. Most folks with a lick of sense sat by the fire and kept home rather than travel these backroads.

Cole had eyes like a hawk and could see anyone coming from a long way off. If they did see someone, he and Snodgrass would slink off into the bushes until they passed. If they did encounter anyone, Snodgrass had promised to do the talking and Cole had promised to do the shooting, but he knew that they'd be better off avoiding trouble in the first place.

The fact that they were heading south again, toward the fighting, didn't seemed to bother Snodgrass. He'd been on his way north to surrender when he'd run into Cole, who talked sense into him and got him turned around again.

"The war ain't over, Snodgrass," Cole had pointed out.

"If we take our time, maybe it will be."

They had run into some bushwhackers just this side of the Potomac who had tried to hang them as deserters. Bushwhackers or Home Guard, call them what you want, they claimed to have the law on their side, only the law was whatever they said. Wasn't no judge or jury, just them and a rope. They'd hang you and then steal whatever you had. Cole had put a stop to that. Those bushwhackers wouldn't bother nobody again until Judgment Day.

He and Snodgrass knew each other from serving in the same unit before Cole had been turned into an assassin. Snodgrass didn't ask after the details, but had agreed to accompany Cole down to City Point on the James River. General Grant and his Army of the Potomac had their headquarters there, readying an attack on Richmond itself. Snodgrass didn't ask what Cole planned to do with that rifle of his once they got there, but Cole reckoned that Snodgrass already knew.

Snodgrass was a natural-born talker and he didn't seem to mind if Cole only grunted once in a while. For his part, Cole felt relieved when a lone farmhouse came into sight because it meant that Snodgrass would shut his pie hole for a while.

The house was a two-story clapboard farmhouse, unpainted, and the structure looked too narrow and tall. The missing rails of the worm fences and the empty pastures leading toward a stand of trees near the road testified to the fact that both armies had picked the place clean. This part of Virginia had seen troops from both sides pass through. Somebody was hanging on here, if just barely. A thin ribbon of smoke rose from the chimney and blew their way.

Cole's pace slowed and he turned to study the woodlot they were passing. The underbrush was thick back in there and trees were mostly swamp maples, their trunks gray and bleak in the winter light.

"What is it?" Snodgrass asked.

"Just keep movin'," Cole spoke quietly, but shifted so that his rifle was pointed in the direction of the woods.

"I reckon the farmers in these parts must be tired of soldiers helping themselves to whatever they want," Snodgrass said quietly, sensing Cole's caution.

Something about the farmhouse beckoned them, however. They had seen the smoke from the chimney. The smoke meant a fire burned in the hearth. If nothing else, it might be a chance to warm up and get the news. With luck, there might even be something to eat. "Let's just see if these folks can spare something," Snodgrass said.

"They won't have much," Cole said doubtfully.

"Well, we got nothin' and next to nothin' is a whole lot more than that," Snodgrass said. Without waiting for Cole, he started up the lane toward the lonely farmhouse.

Cole muttered under his breath and followed. Snodgrass still had too much of the gambler in him, taking chances. But even Cole had to admit that they needed something to eat.

From the looks of the place, Cole knew that these farmers wouldn't have much. The people who clung to these war-torn farms were slowly starving to death. This farm was no exception, judging by its appearance. Hints of whitewash on the buildings and house spoke of better days. Now gray and rickety, the outbuildings looked as if a strong wind would topple them. The fields lay fallow. Clumps of wild multi-flora rose the size of Sibley tents sprouted in the pastures, their bare thorny canes looking witchy and twisted in the gray winter light. The barn roof had holes big enough to throw a cat through.

"Look at them fences, Cole," Snodgrass said, nodding toward what was left of the worm fence that enclosed the pasture. "I reckon the bottom rail done done went to the top."

Cole snorted at the well-worn phrase. Confederate soldiers were forbidden to take more than the top rail of fences for firewood. Of course, the remaining rail was always the top rail, which made it fair game for soldiers without them breaking any rules. Fences did not last long when scavenging soldiers needed firewood.

When they had walked halfway up the lane, a couple of dogs came flying from under the porch and bounded toward them, baying and barking. A boy appeared, coming in from the field beyond the barn. He was toting a gun that was as tall as he was, but he wasn't pointing it at Cole and Snodgrass—not yet, anyhow.

"Where in blazes did he come from?" Snodgrass wondered. He waved to show that they were friendly, hoping that the boy would call the dogs off, but the boy stopped and stood watching them. The dogs came on, barking and howling. Snodgrass got ready to let loose a good kick, but finally the boy whistled. The dogs stopped stood a ways off from Cole and Snodgrass, still barking up a storm. The dogs looked too skinny and their ribs showed.

"You still reckon this is a good idea?" Cole asked.

Snodgrass stepped forward before the boy could get a good look at Cole. With his hard stare, Cole tended to scare people off. He'd tried to tell Cole before that the thing to do was lead off with a compliment. "Those are good dogs, son," Snodgrass said. "They bite?"

"No, sir. They bark is all."

"It's a good dog that lets you know strangers is coming up the road."

The boy came closer, and they got a good look at him. The boy's clothes were hardly more than rags and his coat was so short that the sleeves stopped well up his forearms, exposing wrists and hands that looked raw and red with cold. The coat had so many patches that it was hard to tell where the original coat began. The boy gripped an ancient musket, possibly a flint-lock, but kept it pointed at the ground. The metal looked old and pitted.

"You alone on this place, boy?" Snodgrass asked. Despite the boy's shabby appearance, he still held out some hope of warm kitchen and a plate of hot food.

"No, sir. My mama and sister is in the house."

"What about your pa?"

The boy hesitated. "He'll be back soon. He went into town."

"Uh huh," Snodgrass said. The boy was lying, and all three of them knew it. Snodgrass noticed that the boy couldn't seem to take his eyes off Cole's rifle. The Sharps was shiny and well-oiled, with a brass telescope sight.

Cole's eyes, in turn, were on the barn, where several animal skins had been tacked to dry. They had been stretched to cure with the skin side out. He caught a glimpse of red fur on one, and gray and black on the other. Fox and raccoon hides.

"You done a good job skinning them out, boy," Cole said, speaking for the first time. "You were down in that thicket by the road, watching us, weren't you?"

"Yes, sir." The boy shifted from foot to foot, trying to keep warm. They could see the boy's stockings because he had outgrown his boots, so the toes had been cut out in front to make room.

"It's a smart boy that watches who's coming up the road these days," Cole said. He was glad that the boy hadn't decided to shoot at them. "Now run on up to the house and tell your mama that there's two hungry soldiers here."

Cole's words had brought a faint smile to the boy's face. He turned and ran toward the house, the dogs loping at the boy's house.

"You said he was down in the woods watchin' us, huh," Snodgrass said. "I'm awful glad that he didn't decide to shoot us and nail our hides to that barn."

Cole snorted. "The day ain't done yet, Snodgrass."

No SOONER HAD they started toward the house but the boy's mother came out on the porch. She wore an apron over a thin calico dress and the hands on her hips looked red and raw from work. There wouldn't be any hired help on the farm or servants in this kitchen. Those were working hands. This would be the woman who had mended the boy's clothes so carefully. She had thrown a shawl across her shoulders to keep off the cold. Ten years ago this woman would have been pretty, but hard work and care had etched deep worry lines across her face.

Cole had seen a number of women like this, left to manage a farm and a family while the father was off at war. Such women faced duty hard as any soldier's—if not harder. Her boy had come out on the porch with her and he still held the old rifle. Cole and Snodgrass took off their hats.

"Yankee or Confederate?" the woman asked, no welcoming note in her tone. "I would hazard to say Confederate, seeing the state of your clothes."

Snodgrass stepped forward. "Confederate, ma'am," he said.

"Why ain't you with the army then?" she demanded.

"Ma'am, we've been fightin' with the army for close to four years now so we reckoned it could get on just fine without us for a spell." He added, "We were on furlough and now we are headed back to fight with General Hill down at Petersburg."

Snodgrass put on his best smile, but it struggled in the cold to generate any warmth in return.

"We've got us a Home Guard in these parts that likes to hang people—papers or not. You should keep to the fields during the daytime," she said. The woman's glare faded. "I can tell you that a couple of soldiers as skinny as you two ain't goin' to do General Hill much good. You may as well eat something, and then be on your way. We ain't got much, and that's a fact, but we can spare something."

"Much obliged, ma'am," Snodgrass said, wringing his hat like the neck of a chicken bound for Sunday dinner.

"You may as well come in and get warm while you wait," she added grudgingly. "Leave them muddy boots off on the porch."

With that, the woman and the boy disappeared into the house. They followed after shucking off their boots.

Inside, the kitchen was simple and well-worn, but clean. A farm sink held a pan for washing dishes. Faded gingham curtains at the windows indicated an attempt at brightening the room. The kitchen still had a hearth rather than a cooking stove, and the large brick fireplace dominated the room. An oak mantel stretched the length of the hearth, decorated with a few plates. The mantel also held two oil lamps with globes that had already been cleaned after last night's use, indicating that this was an efficient household. Two empty pegs above the hearth showed where a firearm would normally hang—likely the old gun still in the boy's hands.

"Jesse, put that gun up," she said, then looked at the two men. "No guns at the table."

"Yes, ma'am," Snodgrass said politely. Cole and Snodgrass set their weapons aside.

"Set yourselves down," the woman said. "I've got some stew here. Hope you like squirrel. Game is about the only meat we got these days. The soldiers on the road took the rest—or that Home Guard. They're the worst ones, truth be told, and they're what passes for the law around here."

"The stew smells right good, ma'am," Snodgrass said. He seemed to have elected himself spokesman. Not that Cole minded. He never had been much for talking to folks. He pulled up a chair, noticing how much his belly rumbled at the smell of good cooking. "I'm Uriah Snodgrass, by the way. This here quiet one is Lucas Cole."

"I am Mrs. Hartley," the woman said. "Mr. Hartley is off with General Lee, last I heard, defending Richmond. You done met my boy, Jesse."

"You shoot that squirrel, Jesse?" Cole asked.

"Yes, sir."

Cole nodded. "Thought so. I reckon we have you to thank as much as your mama here."

Jesse sat up straighter as if Cole had just pinned a medal on him.

They heard a noise upstairs that had both Cole and Snodgrass looking toward their guns.

"That's Lorena," Mrs. Hartley said. "She's most likely putting on her best dress."

"I am not!" came a loud voice from the kitchen doorway, where a pretty young girl of about nineteen stood, smoothing down her dress. Cole saw that the cloth was threadbare and that the dress could never compare to the finery that he had seen back in Washington City. However, a young girl could wear a gunny sack and still be a sight to behold. Lorena had her mother's dark hair and similar features. Mrs. Hartley must have been a handsome woman before the war and the farm had worn her down.

Cole and Snodgrass stood, pushing back awkwardly from the table.

"Sit down now and eat your stew," Mrs. Hartley ordered. "Lorena, ain't no need to make a fuss."

Cole turned his attention to the steaming bowl set before him. A plate of cornpone sat nearby. He appreciated that Mrs. Hartley had shared the family's meager victuals. He noticed that

Snodgrass had not given his undivided attention to the stew, but kept stealing glances at Lorena.

Mrs. Harley also noticed those glances. She cleared her throat and said, "Lorena, fetch me a bucket of water from the well."

"Why can't Jesse do it?"

"She can't make me do everything!" Jesse protested.

Cole spoke up. "I'll fetch the water, ma'am. It's the least I can do after that stew."

Mrs. Hartley was glaring at Lorena, apparently ready to say something to her daughter, but bit back her words. Cole had a way of speaking that closed the door on any argument.

"I'll help you," young Jesse said, jumping up.

"That would be might fine of you, Jesse," Cole said.

Leaving Snodgrass to take his chances with the two women in the kitchen, he and the boy went out to the yard, following the well-worn path to the well. Jesse had brought along a wooden piggin to fill with well water.

"My pa dug this well," Jesse said as Cole raised a bucket of water. "He said he'd found the sweetest water around."

"Good water," Cole agreed, sampling it with a dipper that hung there. "How long has your pa been gone?"

"Two years, I reckon," Jesse said. "Ma ain't had a letter from him in a while."

"I'm sure he'll write when he can," Cole said. A man wouldn't write home for any number of reasons, not the least of which was that he was dead. Cole didn't say as much to the boy, but Jesse must have some idea about that. The boy seemed wise beyond his years. This hard life had forced him to grow up fast. Something about the boy reminded Cole of himself. He was also glad that the boy would be too young to fight in the war.

Cole carried the water back into the kitchen. He ducked back out and returned with an armload of wood for the fire. He saw that Snodgrass had hardly noticed him coming and going because he only had eyes for Lorena.

"You are surely useful to have around, Mr. Cole," Mrs. Hartley said. "Jesse won't have no chores left."

"Like I said, ma'am, it's the least we can do."

Mrs. Hartley nodded, as if she had just reached some decision. "Dark comes early and it's fixin' to be a cold night. You and Mr. Snodgrass are welcome to spend the night in the barn. We can send you on your way in the morning, after you get something to eat."

"We thank you kindly for that, ma'am."

Cole slept with his rifle close, just in case Mrs. Hartley was friendlier with the Home Guard than she let on.

DAYLIGHT TOOK its time on winter mornings. Both Cole and Snodgrass slept later than they had intended in the relative warmth of the barn. Lorena woke them up, coming in to milk the cow and clanging the bucket against the stall. She had brought along her brother, Cole suspected at her mother's urging, so that she would have a chaperone.

"Ain't you goin' to help me?" Lorena called up to the loft. Cole looked at Snodgrass, who shrugged, and climbed down the ladder to help milk the cow. To Cole's eye, the bony old cow looked to be stingy with her milk, but she was the family's only cow.

In less than a minute, it became clear that Snodgrass was no farmer. Snodgrass was a rarity in the Confederate army in that he had not been a farmer before the war. The ranks held some tradesmen, along with a newspaper editor or schoolteacher now and then, but even most of them had some experience with milking. Snodgrass was more familiar with dealing cards. It was a wonder that he had volunteered to milk the cow, but Miss Lorena possessed enough charm for a man to be willing to make a fool of himself.

The old cow shifted sideways and sent Snodgrass sprawling on the straw-covered barn floor.

"That ain't how you milk a cow!" Lorena cried, beside herself with laughter. Her younger brother was doubled over at the sight. "You got to be gentle with Bessie."

"Bessie was none too gentle with me," Snodgrass complained.

"Try it again."

"You show me how," Snodgrass said.

Lorena retrieved the stool and empty bucket that Snodgrass had managed to scatter when the cow tipped him over. She sat down on the stool, running her hand reassuringly along the cow's flank. She took hold of the udders and began working them in such a way that streams of milk shot into the bucket.

"See? It ain't that hard."

Snodgrass laughed. "So you say."

Snodgrass noticed Cole sitting on the edge of the loft, legs dangling, and enjoying the show. He glared up at him and said, "Don't just stand there and watch. You could muck out a stall or something."

"That seems like just about the right job for you now that you're practically a farmer," Cole replied.

Once the milking was done, the four of them walked up to the house. Mrs. Hartley was setting out a plate of biscuits and some beans, along with a tin pot of coffee. Cole had brought in an armload of wood from outside, and he stacked it neatly beside the stove.

"Thank you kindly," Mrs. Hartley said.

"Least we could do," Cole said quietly.

"This looks delicious, ma'am," Snodgrass said.

Busying herself around the kitchen, Mrs. Hartley replied, "It's a poor meal that doesn't have some meat."

"We're grateful all the same, ma'am," Cole said.

"We ought to go get us that hog I seen in the woods," Jesse said.

Mrs. Hartley shook her head. "If you miss, that hog is half-wild and mean as a bee-stung bull. We don't need meat that bad."

"I ain't gonna miss!" Jesse said.

Mrs. Hartley pointed her wooden spoon at him. "Jesse Hartley, you mind you don't sass me."

"Yes, ma'am."

Cole looked at the boy. "After these biscuits, let's go see how you shoot."

Young Jesse could barely contain his excitement, but Cole managed to down two biscuits, some beans, and a hot cup of coffee. Then they headed back outside, with only Mrs. Hartley staying behind in the kitchen.

A handful of stumps stood at one end of a field that Mr. Hartley had cleared before going off to war. Cole had Jesse run down and put a bottle on one of these stumps. Cole asked the boy, "Reckon you can hit that bottle?"

"That's kind of far," the boy said. The bottle looked awfully small from this distance.

"Let's see," Cole replied.

Jesse shouldered the rifle, took careful aim, finally squeezed off a shot. The bottle remained unscathed as the echo of the shot crashed away through the low hills.

"Dammit!" Jesse exclaimed.

"Jesse Hartley!" Lorena admonished him. "You best watch you don't use such language around mama."

Jesse ignored his big sister and looked up at Cole.

"Mind your sister, now," Cole said. "Cussin' won't break that bottle. Go ahead and reload."

Cole was impressed at how quickly the boy was able to take a paper cartridge from his coat pocket, tear it open with his teeth, and pour the charge down the barrel of the old gun. The boy rammed the load home and had the percussion cap in place as fast as any veteran.

"I'll get it this time," the boy vowed.

"It's hard to hit anything from a standing position," Cole

said. "Whenever you can, put the rifle across something to steady it. A fence, a stump, a rock. Then you don't have to hold the weight of the rifle. All you have to do is aim."

"No stumps around here," Snodgrass pointed out. They stood in the open part of the field.

"Then you lie on the ground like this," Cole said, getting on his belly in the dry winter grass. He propped his elbows on the ground and spread his legs out behind him. "Get on down here, boy."

Jesse got down and Cole helped him get his elbows into place. "Easier," the boy agreed.

"Let your breath out, then take in a deep breath and hold it. Keep your finger on that trigger and squeeze it real gentle."

Seconds went by as the boy followed Cole's instructions. Finally, the rifle fired. At the other end of the field, the bottle shattered.

"I hit it!" Jesse sounded surprised.

"There you go," Cole said.

"I'll bet you can shoot a bottle from even farther away," the boy said. "Let me go put another bottle on that stump."

"Ain't my day to shoot," Cole said.

Cole got up and dusted himself off. He felt pleased that the boy had hit the bottle at this distance. He hoped that all this boy would ever have to shoot were bottles and varmints.

"Gettin' cold out here," Snodgrass said. "Let's go see if there's any of that hot coffee left."

"You go on," Cole said. "I reckon that there's more than one way to warm up."

Once they returned to the house, Cole stopped outside the door at the wood pile and picked up the ax. He tested the edge with a well-practiced thumb. "This here ax is dull. You got a grindstone?"

"Out in the barn," Jesse said.

"Come on, then. Let me show you how to keep this ax sharp. Chopping wood with a dull ax is twice as much work."

The two headed toward the barn. Snodgrass watched them go, shaking his head. He knew Cole for a hard man, but here he was teaching the boy to shoot and how to sharpen an ax.

Lorena was also watching them go, a wistful smile on her face. "Jesse misses pa," she said. "Your friend could be Jesse's older brother. He's handy on the farm."

"Cole is a lot of things," Snodgrass said.

A little while later, they heard the sound of chopping outside the door and Jesse began to run in and out of the kitchen with armloads of wood, filling the rack beside the stove to overflowing. Cole didn't stop for an hour, when he came in for coffee. Snodgrass went out to the barn to get a shirt he wanted to pay Mrs. Hartley to mend, leaving Cole alone with Lorena and Mrs. Hartley while Jesse brought in more wood. Cole was almost finished with the coffee when Jesse burst in.

"There's soldiers comin' up the road!" he cried.

Cole was already out of the chair. "Yankees or Confederates?"

"Home Guard," Jesse said. He went for the old rifle in the corner. "Last time, they took two chickens."

Cole took the rifle from Jesse and returned it to the corner. "Guns will only make trouble," he said. His own rifle was out in the barn, along with Snodgrass. He hoped that Snodgrass had the good sense to stay out of sight. Cole couldn't reach the barn without being seen.

"Upstairs," Mrs. Hartley said.

Cole nodded and went up the steps two at a time. He found three rooms upstairs, sparsely furnished.

Before he slid under the bed in what must be Jesse's room, he chanced a peek out the window. The riders had already reached the farm. He counted five men, wearing a patchwork of butternut uniforms. Some of the men had white hair and beards, indicating that they were too old to be soldiering. Definitely Home Guard. But without anyone to question their authority, groups of men such as this ran roughshod over the small farms across the South, worse than any marauding Yankees.

If he'd had his rifle, Cole could have gotten a few of them as they rode in and evened the odds. However, that would only bring trouble down on the Hartleys. He got under the bed and hoped that Snodgrass stayed out of the way and that the boy didn't do anything foolish.

Beneath him, he felt the house tremble and the scrape of boots as some of the men entered. He heard their voices clearly just a few feet below.

"Captain Corliss," Mrs. Hartley said, a nervous edge to her voice. It occurred to him that maybe he had put too much faith in the woman. At a word from her, these Home Guard riders would stretch Cole's and Snodgrass's necks. She had nothing to gain from hiding them, and everything to lose. But all that Mrs. Hartley said next was, "Ain't seen you in a spell."

"We was out on a patrol and I thought that we would pay you a visit. We have had reports of deserters on the road. I wanted to make sure that you were safe, considerin' that you are out here all alone."

"Alone? Why, I have my son and daughter here, Captain," she said. "That's more than enough. Lorena, fetch Captain Corliss a cup of hot coffee, then bring the pot out to his men. Jesse, you help your sister."

"Much obliged," Corliss said. Several long moments passed when Cole heard only silence as the Home Guard officer apparently drank his coffee. "Ma'am, have you seen any men on the road?"

"If I had, Captain, I believe that I would have said so by now."

Corliss grunted. "You can't be too careful these days," he said. The metal cup clicked down on the table. "They say that some of our boys have gotten discouraged and are headed home, never mind that the war ain't over and that they're still soldiers. Desertion is a hangin' offense, ma'am."

"So I've heard."

"How you gettin' on? With your husband away and all?"

"Good as we can, I reckon," Mrs. Hartley said. "Thank you for your concern, Captain. Does this mean you won't be taking any chickens this time?"

"Those were for the war effort. You want to do your part, don't you?"

Mrs. Hartley did not answer that, but said, "We won't starve, not with Jesse out shootin' squirrels."

"Well, that explains it. We heard some shots as we come up the road earlier. I was a mite curious."

"That was Jesse. That's his gun in the corner. He wanted to get it when he heard horses on the road, but I told him to leave it be."

"The men do get nervous," Corliss said. The coffee mug clicked down again. "Thank you kindly for the coffee, ma'am. We'll only take three chickens this time."

"Last time, you took two!"

Corliss did not respond, but Cole heard his boots scrape again on the threshold. Soon, he heard the cackling hens as they protested being scooped up and tied to a saddle by their feet.

Once the horses rode off, Cole came back down the stairs. Mrs. Hartley stood in the kitchen, so angry that her face was pale.

"They rode off with the last of my chickens, and lord knows what else," she said. "It's not right, Corliss and his men taking what they want like that with no one to stop them. They'll be on to the Widow Smith's place next, and she has even less to live on."

"Were those all of Corliss's men?" Cole asked.

"All five of them," Jesse said. "You could fight them, Cole!"

"Jesse!" Mrs. Hartley admonished her son.

Cole didn't say anything else, but he was thinking. Snodgrass appeared at the back door, carrying their two blanket rolls and Cole's rifle. "I hid out in the barn until they rode off," he said. "I brought our things in case we have to skedaddle. It's only going to mean trouble for the Hartleys if that Home Guard finds us here."

Mrs. Hartley snorted. "Home Guard ain't what to call them. They're more like thieves."

Cole nodded. "Snodgrass is right. If that Corliss gets suspicious and circles back, he and his men will hang us. Then, they'll have an excuse to take every last scrap from your place, right down to that old cow."

"Not Bessie!" Lorena said.

Cole looked at Mrs. Hartley. "Ma'am, thank you kindly for all you done and for the meals. It's time for me and Snodgrass to go, just in case those men come back."

"I can't say that we weren't glad of the company," she said, then hurried about the kitchen, wrapping up a few biscuits and some salt pork for them in a scrap of cloth. "It ain't much, but you'll have something for tonight."

"Thank you, ma'am," Cole said. He looked around at the Hartleys, standing there in the kitchen. The mother stood straight as a ramrod, while Lorena kept her eyes on Snodgrass. Jesse stared down at the floor. On an impulse, Cole reached out and tousled his hair. Cole's father had done that to him, back when Cole was a boy. Jesse smiled. "You take care of your mama and sister now, you hear?"

Without another word, he and Snodgrass stepped out into the cold, the door closing behind them. The wintry Virginia countryside looked even more bleak and brown than usual. The murky sky spit a few grains of sleet at them. They slipped their blanket rolls over their shoulders. Snodgrass started up the lane toward the road, but Cole stopped him. "This way," he said, and set off at a trot across the barren fields.

"Do you mind tellin' me where we're goin'?" Snodgrass asked, panting hard as he struggled to keep up.

"Come on," Cole said.

After nearly a mile, they crossed the fields and cut through the same copse of trees where Jesse had watched them come up the road the other day. The road took the long way around, but Cole and Snodgrass had taken the shortcut. Riding toward them were the five graybeards from the Home Guard, who hadn't seen them yet in the trees beside the road. Sleet fell harder and faster now, causing the men to keep their faces turned down out of the wind.

"Cole, what are you fixin' to do?" Snograss asked, sounding worried.

"Get your pistol out," Cole said.

Cole set the Sharps rifle across a fallen log, with Snodgrass beside him. The log offered good cover and the riders didn't see them as they came even with their hiding place. Cole's first shot knocked Corliss clean out of the saddle. As he reloaded the single-shot Sharps, he heard Snodgrass mutter a curse and start firing the revolver. At this range, even Snodgrass couldn't miss.

Another man went down. Two of the riders wheeled in front of him, firing blindly at the woods now that they realized this was an ambush. They had trouble controlling their horses, whirling around like two drunks dancing the Virginia reel. Cole waited until one man was behind the other, then pulled the trigger. The big slug from the Sharps hit them both.

That left one man. He jerked at the reins, turning his horse to make a run for it, but Snodgrass leveled the pistol at him and brought the man down with his last shot.

Cole slipped the sling of the Sharps over his shoulder and drew his own revolver. The two men that he had taken down with the same bullet struggled to get up, badly wounded but still alive. Cole shot them both. He walked over to Corliss and saw the eyes staring blankly. Corliss's hat had flown off when he'd been shot and flecks of sleet gathered in the dead man's beard and hair.

Snodgrass moved to catch two of the horses that hadn't run off. One of the horses had the three chickens still tied to the saddle. He set two of them free on the unlikely chance that they would find their way home and kept one for supper. "What the hell was that all about?" he asked.

"Snodgrass, that Home Guard was just goin' to go back to the Hartleys and take more and more," he said. "Hell, do you think Lorena was safe with them around? I couldn't shoot them back at the farm because it would make trouble for the Hartleys. Now, it looks like they done run into some deserters."

"A mile from the Hartley place? Cole, they'll know we done it."

"The Hartleys might guess," Cole agreed. "Ain't nobody else gonna be the wiser."

Snodgrass shook his head. "Well, at least we can ride their horses."

"We have an open road ahead of us, too. No more Home Guard to worry about."

"Until the next bunch," Snodgrass said.

Cole slapped the rifle. "We'll deal with them when the time comes."

"I was afraid you would say that."

Cole swung into the saddle. "The war ain't over for us, Snodgrass, not by a long sight. I just hope it's over for the Hartleys."

They wheeled the horses and rode off at a trot, finally disappearing around a bend, leaving five dead men in the road.

STORY ADAPTED from an unpublished chapter of *Sharpshooter*, Berkley Books, 1999.

GRAY GHOSTS

The soldiers rode up just after mid-morning, catching Louisa halfway between the back door and the spring-house, where she had a nice crock of sweet butter keeping cool. It was one of those mornings where the mist clings to the edges of the woods and in the hollows, and at first the riders appeared like gray ghosts to Louisa.

They wore ragged uniforms and the dust of the road hung about them like an aura, adding to their ethereal appearance. But then one of them coughed on the dust and another shifted in his saddle so that the leather creaked. They were men, all right, not phantoms. Confederate cavalry. The country lane past the farm-house was not much used except by the local farmers, so the sight of the rebels was most unusual. Despite the rising late June heat, Louisa felt frozen in place.

"Ma'am," said the rebel with the gold braid on his sleeves, tipping his plumed hat with a gloved hand. A fine shower of dust shook from the feather.

"You're a rebel," she managed to say, as if the soldiers did not know what they were. Her heart was pounding. She wondered where her husband, Samuel, had gone to—he should be out here, protecting her, holding his pistol on these men.

"Yes ma'am," the officer said. "I'm Captain Asher. We're with J.E.B. Stuart's cavalry, assigned to the Army of Northern Virginia."

"Rebels," she repeated. "All the way out here."

Generally, this area of Maryland had been spared by the war, with most of the action taking place closer to the Potomac River several miles away. Loyalties remained divided here, and it wasn't unheard of for local men to have slipped across that river to fight for the South. That was one thing—Confederates in one's yard was quite another. There were rumors of troops moving on the Washington Road nearby, but Rebel cavalry was certainly the last thing she had expected to encounter this morning.

Louisa's horrified expression made the captain stir uncomfortably in his saddle. Looking more closely at him, she could see that all the dust and sunburn, along with his cavalier manner, hid that fact that he was quite young.

"We're not here to harm anyone, ma'am," he said, suddenly sounding as young as he looked. "Just to forage for supplies."

She felt some of her fear solidifying into anger. "You mean you're here to steal from us."

"No, ma'am. We're under orders to pay for everything we take." The captain patted a saddlebag. "In Confederate currency, of course."

"Which is just about worthless," Louisa snapped at him. "Why, it's not worth the paper it's printed on."

At Louisa's sharp words, there was just a glimmer of anger in the rebel's blue eyes. Louisa wondered if she had gone too far. Where was Samuel? Louisa had been on her way to the springhouse when the rebels rode up; Samuel must still be in the house. Surely, he must have seen the rebels by now. She wanted him to appear right now and confront these thieves, sending them on their way with their tails between their legs. She wouldn't mind at all if Samuel came out shooting, mowing them all down with his pistol. But Louisa knew that wasn't going to happen. It was not Samuel's way. He'd be peering out a window, biding his time, thinking that she was handling the situation perfectly.

It was as if the Confederate captain could read her mind. "You alone here?" he asked, not looking at her but at the house. Some of the polite tone had gone out of his voice after Louisa's comments. He shouldn't be surprised, she thought; not everyone in Maryland was a Southern sympathizer who would welcome these feral cavalrymen.

"No, I'm not alone," she said hurriedly. She nodded at the new center-gable cottage nearby—two rooms downstairs and three upstairs, with a kitchen lean-to off the back. "My husband is in the house."

"If you say so, ma'am ," the Confederate said. He shifted in the saddle, the leather creaking. "You reckon he won't mind us having a look around?"

"I'm sure he does mind," said Louisa, who was wondering with ever-increasing apprehension just what had become of her husband. Was he cowering in the parlor? "Why don't you go on up to the house and ask him?"

But the Confederate captain appeared to forget all about the house, apparently having decided that Louis was lying about not being alone. She wouldn't have been the first woman they had encountered left to fend for herself on the farm. Instead, he turned in the saddle and gave orders to his men. "All right, boys, let's get to it. You know what to do. Hollis, you ride down and check the barn and the springhouse, see if there's anything in them."

Louisa's mind filled with a sudden, horrible image of leaping flames. "Are you going to burn the place?" she asked.

The officer blinked down at her from atop his horse, a smile showing through the dusty beard. He had thought that Louisa was speaking in jest. "No, ma'am," he finally said, seeing that she was serious. "That ain't generally what we do."

The soldiers set about ransacking the outbuildings and barns with the methodical approach of men who had done this many times before. Most of the time it was like a game; the farmer had something to hide, where had he hidden it? The rebels stayed away from the house, and it was clear to Louisa that they were after livestock and foodstuffs, not the sort of valuables a house might contain. Louisa immediately saw the logic of this, because a soldier wouldn't have much use for furniture and books.

"Whooee! Git 'em, Silas!" one of the rebels shouted in encouragement as another man chased the chickens. The men laughed as Silas caught a hen, then another. There were only four chickens, as Samuel and Louisa had been fighting a losing battle all spring with a fox who lived in the woods below the barn. The soldier tied up the hens by their feet and tossed them over the rump of his horse, where they fluttered and protested to no avail. The hens looked just how Louisa felt.

Down at the barn, Hollis emerged with a sack of oats on his shoulder. Louisa felt a pang as she saw another man coming out of the barn, leading the gray mare that Louisa and Samuel used to pull their carriage from the train station at Sykesville. Their dutiful, quiet mare would not last long in Confederate service, she thought.

"Ain't much here," Hollis shouted.

It was true. After all, she and Samuel weren't farmers. The house in the country was simply a summer getaway for them. They would survive the loss of some chickens and a bag of oats and their gray mare. However, some of their neighbors had rich farms thanks to the fertile soil of western Howard County. Their neighbors had barnyards full of fat hogs, well-lardered smoke-houses, and horses. For them, this foraging raid by the rebels would be devastating, the payment of worthless Confederate currency no consolation for the fact that their families might starve come winter.

"Is this all you have, ma'am?" the young officer asked, seeming puzzled as he surveyed the modest yard. "If you hid your livestock, we'll find it, you can rest assured."

"We're not farmers," Louisa explained. "Even the crops in

the fields aren't ours. The land is rented out to a tenant. This is our summer house."

"Summer house?" The captain didn't appear to understand.

"We come out here to the country to escape the heat in Baltimore. My husband works for the B&O Railroad and we take the train out to Sykesville. It's just a short wagon ride to the depot."

Captain Asher nodded, although he now looked bemused. It was clear that he was taken with the concept of a summer house. In his world, there would only be the war. Trooper Hollis approached him with a cavalryman's bowlegged shuffle.

"All we got is four chickens, that little mare and a bag of oats," Hollis said, tallying the soldier's efforts. "There's also some beets in the garden back here. Ain't much."

Louisa felt a sharp comment coming to her lips at this man's assessment of her possessions that he was stealing, but she let it die away. For some reason, Louisa felt it was important now not to antagonize the rebels. They were the enemy, after all; they killed Yankees, and the farm was far away from any help. She was beginning to think that it was wise not to test Captain Asher's sense of chivalry any more than necessary. She wished that she hadn't said anything about them burning the place for fear that she might be putting ideas in their heads.

Some of the men were getting back on their horses and their sabers clanked and rattled. It was a martial sound that seemed out of place at her country getaway. On several of the tattered uniforms she saw stains that looked like blood. The humid mist had not lifted and the air felt still and close, filled with the smell of lathered horses, damp saddle leather, and men's sweat. She was glad that they were preparing to ride out. At the same time, she understood that the sight of Confederate troops in her yard was not something that she was likely ever to see again. She had seen Union cavalry passing in the road and they were far better equipped—and cleaner—than these Confederates. They were like smoke and oakum, she thought, slipping down the dusty roads and fields. She felt her sense of outrage fade.

"You'll ride past the springhouse on your way. There's a crock of sweet butter in there and some milk," she volunteered. She could not resist adding, "You may as well have them too, seeing how you've taken everything else."

"Thank you for your kind hospitality, ma'am," Captain Asher said, doffing his dusty, wide-brimmed hat and making an exaggerated bow from the saddle.

His impertinence infuriated her once more, but Louisa bit back the retort that came to her tongue, reminding herself that these soldiers could yet prove dangerous. She watched the captain reach into his saddlebag and thrust a handful of bills at her, not bothering to count it. It was clear the captain didn't have any confidence in the value of Confederate money, either, but was doling it out by the handful. Louisa took the bills and clenched them in her fist; with an effort she resisted the urge to toss them in the dirt or hurl them back at the captain. She just wanted the soldiers gone.

"We'll be on our way," the captain said, and he slowly turned his horse into the road, heading downhill toward the barn and the springhouse. Several of the other raiders had already moved out; she watched as the one named Hollis came to the springhouse, dismounted, and disappeared inside. He emerged moments later with his arms laden with the milk and butter. Her chicken flapped weakly behind Hollis's saddle and another rebel was leading off their little gray carriage horse.

She was glad to see the backs of them, truth be told. However, the next farm the rebels would reach was the Crook place, about a mile down the winding road through the woods. The Crooks were not playing at being farmers like she and Samuel but lived off what they grew and raised on their modest acreage. She imagined the desperate look Martha Crook would have on her face as the soldiers carried off her chickens and livestock. Mrs. Crook was a widow—her husband had died fighting for the Union and now her two older boys helped her run the farm. The soldiers would take everything the Crooks had of any value, which wasn't much, but they needed it to survive. Martha Crook had many mouths to feed.

With that thought in mind, Louis turned and walked toward the house, lifting the bottom of her skirt so that it wouldn't drag in the dust. Her mouth twisted as she thought of what she would be saying to her husband, who had not shown himself at all during the encounter with the rebels.

Finally, Samuel stepped out onto the back porch. He held a pistol limply in his right hand, which dangled at his side. He was an almost regal man in many ways: tall and handsome, with dark hair that curled just a bit over his collar, and always well-dressed even here on the farm. No one would ever mistake his clothes for a farmer's, although he was as well-built as any of the farmers who gathered to meet the train in Sykesville. He glanced at his wife, then beyond her where the road led into the woods. "They're gone," he announced.

"I know that," Louisa snapped. "What were you doing in here with that pistol? The soldiers never came near the house."

"If I had gone outside with this pistol in my hand those soldiers would have shot me down," he said matter-of-factly. "Of course, if they had insulted you in any way, I would have come out."

She realized her husband was simply being practical. It was just like him to lurk in the house with a pistol but not to show himself and stand up to the rebels. That same pragmatism had made him a successful executive of the Baltimore and Ohio Railroad, which had suffered much from the war. It had been the railroad's strategy not to interfere against marauding raiders but simply to repair the damage as a cost of doing business. Louisa swallowed a biting comment. Where was the man's emotion? She was his wife, after all, not some holding of the railroad company.

"We need to warn the Crooks," she said.

"How are we going to do that?" he asked. "The soldiers have a head start on us."

"Give me your pistol," she said.

"Louisa?"

"I said, give it here."

He handed it over. Using two hands, she cocked the revolver and pointed it at the sky. Samuel had taught her how to shoot; out here in the country there were snakes aplenty and the occasional marauding fox bothering the chickens. The neighbors would have said, though, that a pistol was a city weapon. Out here in the countryside, shotguns were the firearm of choice.

She fired, doing a tolerable job of keeping the pistol steady as it bucked in her grip, then cocked the hammer and fired again. And again. Three shots was the universal warning. Ears ringing, she handed the still-smoking pistol back to Samuel after the third shot. "Now Martha Crook will know something's wrong."

"She'll probably send one of her boys over here to see what the shooting was about."

"And if he meets the rebels on the road he can run home and warn his mother."

Together, they turned and went back into the house. They had hardly closed the door when they heard the sharp cracks of distant pistol shots and the flat bang of muskets.

Louisa blanched and ran to the window, peering through the wavy glass. The trees obscured her view, but she could hear the firing and a few shouts. Not that far off. "My God, Samuel, they're fighting in the woods."

"Get away from the window," he said, taking her by the hand and leading her deeper into the house.

Here, they would be protected from any stray bullets by the horsehair plaster walls of the farmhouse. The firing went on hotly for another few minutes, then ended with a few scattered shots.

"Do you think the Crooks are all right?" Louisa asked, although she didn't imagine for a minute that Martha Crook and her gaggle of youngsters had ambushed the Confederates. The foraging party must have run into the local militia.

"It didn't sound as if the firing was as far as their farm," Samuel said. "Those rebels ran into somebody in the woods, from the sounds of it, probably near where the road crosses the creek."

Louisa knew the place well because it was the same narrow country road that they followed to and from the railroad depot. Samuel had a habit of speaking to her with the same authority that he used on railroad employees and that tone annoyed her at the best of times. Already fraught with emotion, she couldn't keep quiet anymore.

"You certainly know a lot about soldiering for a man who hides in the house while his wife confronts an entire Confederate raiding party in the yard," she said.

Samuel glowered at her, started to open his mouth to speak, then seemed to think better of it and clamped his lips tight. He turned and went out on the front porch. She heard his boots pacing back and forth on the wooden floorboards, and then the scrape of a match as he lit a cigar. Knowing Samuel, he would stay out there, brooding, until suppertime.

She regretted saying anything. As usual, she had gotten herself into trouble by speaking before she could think it through. Her quick tongue was exactly what had nearly turned the courteous Confederate captain into a hostile enemy soldier; now, she had made her husband angry. She had gone too far.

Samuel was a good man, and she knew he was right about the foolish gesture that confronting the soldiers in the yard with his pistol would have been. The rebels might have shot him. A horrible image came to mind of Samuel lying bleeding in the yard. The very thought made Louisa shudder.

They had come to their summer house in the countryside to escape the heat of the city, and also the war, which had caused endless problems in the operation of the B&O as first one side and then the other swept across the tracks in western Maryland.

Some sections of track had changed hands several times, and the railroad was left with the constant aggravation of rebuilding the burned bridges and repairing the damaged rails that armies always left in their wakes. Today, however, the war had found them on their hideaway farm.

It seemed that there was no escaping the war that was now dragging on. Louisa had always thought it was odd that her husband had not enlisted. He was still young enough for field duty, even though he had a stiff knee that gave him trouble on long walks, and with his connections he would easily receive an officer's commission. There was even a good chance he could serve in Baltimore, or even in Washington City, just a short train ride away. She didn't want her husband killed or even put in danger—she had no interest in being a young widow like poor Martha Crook—but there was a respectability Louisa missed in not being able to say her husband was serving the Union.

However, Samuel had never shown an interest in going off to war. Whenever she asked Samuel why he didn't enlist, he always said he was busy enough helping the war effort with his job on the railroad. As the war entered its third summer, the fact that Samuel would not put on a uniform had become something of an issue between them, although it was largely unspoken. Louisa did not like to think of her husband as a coward, but she was beginning to wonder if that might just be the case. Would a real man have hidden in the house while his wife confronted those riders?

Still, the morning's events had been jarring enough; she didn't want them to spend the rest of the day at odds with each other. She went out on the porch. He leaned stiffly against a porch railing, smoking a cigar and staring off across the field of wildflowers and orchard grass that served as a front lawn. "Samuel, I am sorry for what I said. I did not mean it."

"Yes, you did." He wouldn't look at her, but blew a cloud of cigar smoke toward the big hill to the west of the farm. "We'll catch the train for Baltimore in the morning, and I'll enlist in the army. Ted Hughes wants me in his regiment; he's already said he would get me a commission as major."

"You don't have to enlist to prove anything to me."

"It's what you've wanted, I know."

"I don't want you to join the army."

"That's not true, Louisa, and we both know it. I'll be wearing a uniform as soon as we get to the city tomorrow."

With that, he tossed away the remains of his cigar and went back into the house, abandoning the porch to her. After all this time, she knew she should be glad at the news that he would finally enlist, but Samuel was too bitter for her to take any joy in his decision. She wanted him to join the army for himself, not because of her own wishes.

She was about to go into the house and try to talk some sense into Samuel when something down the hill caught her eye. Coming up the road out of the woods was the party of Confederate cavalry that had made off with her chickens and butter. They were still leading the mare at the end of a rope.

Louisa had been brave once today, but the sight of the gray riders returning was too much for her. Her emotions had been strained enough. With a sharp intake of breath, she watched them pass the springhouse, and then the barn. One of them appeared to be slumped in the saddle. Once she was certain the soldiers were following the dirt road back up the hill toward the house, Louisa, turned and ran inside.

"Samuel, the rebels are coming back!" she cried.

"What?" This time, there was nothing pragmatic in his tone. He sounded angry. Perhaps he was already thinking like a Union officer. Samuel rarely swore, but he did so now. "Damn them!"

"They're coming back up the road!"

He went out on the front porch to see for himself, then came back inside to fetch his pistol. Louisa tried to stop him, realizing all at once how right he had been about not confronting the rebels the first time they had been on the farm. "Samuel, they'll shoot you."

"Let them try, I say! I've had enough of these rebel soldiers riding through our farm."

"Samuel, please—"

He shoved right past her and went out on the porch. Outside, she could hear the jingling of harness and a horse blowing, which meant that the rebels were already in the yard. Louisa choked back a sob, expecting to hear the sound of gunfire as the rebels shot Samuel down. It was all her fault. She had shamed him into it, accused him of being a coward—

"No!" She cried out and ran onto the porch. Samuel stood there, his handsome features twisted in rage, the pistol in his hand leveled at the soldiers. Louisa hurried over and tried to stand close to him, thinking that the rebels might not shoot a woman, but he pushed her roughly behind him, keeping the pistol on the rebels.

"What do you want now?" Samuel demanded. "You have already taken enough."

None of the soldiers spoke up. Several held carbines loosely across their saddles or else with the butt of the stock balanced on their thighs and the muzzles pointed skyward. It would only take an instant for those gun barrels to swing down on Samuel, but the soldiers were not threatening to shoot. Slowly, Samuel lowered the pistol until it hung straight down by his side.

Only then did he and Louisa notice the wounded captain, slumped over in his saddle but still upright, wincing in pain. Blood ran down his leg and dripped off his right boot, spattering in the dust like the first drops of a summer rain.

"Oh," Louisa said, covering her mouth in shock at the sight of the blood.

"Some militia caught us in the woods," the trooper named Hollis explained. "We ran them off, but not before they shot the captain."

"How bad is he?" Samuel asked.

No one answered. In the silence, they could hear the horses chomping their bits. The captain groaned.

"He can't ride," Hollis said. He paused, then took off his hat, revealing tangled hair matted with sweat. "Ma'am, I can see you are a kind person, for all of your fire. We was wondering if we could leave him here—if you folks would care for him."

"You boys go on," Captain Asher said through teeth clenched tightly against the pain. "There's bound to be more Yankee militia around here and in bigger numbers than what we ran into. You all need to get back with the rest of the regiment."

Louisa stepped down off the porch. "Help him off the horse," she heard herself say. Samuel looked at her in surprise, but she went on, "There's a sofa he can lie on in the front parlor. Just let me fetch some blankets."

Suddenly, the porch and yard were a flurry of motion as several troopers dismounted to help the captain off his horse and carry him inside. Samuel caught her by the arm as she turned to go into the house.

"What are you doing?" he demanded in a harsh whisper. "These men come here, steal our chickens and horse like common thieves, and you invite them inside? They are the enemy, Louisa."

Louisa was almost as puzzled by her actions as her husband, but she attempted to explain herself. "Can't you see that he's wounded, Samuel?" she said in hushed tones so the Confederate soldiers nearby wouldn't overhear. "Besides, you are the one with the pistol. If you don't want them here, order them to leave."

Scowling, he let go of her arm and followed her into the house.

Louisa put an old quilt down on the sofa in an attempt to save it from the blood and dirt. The rebels gently laid their captain on top of the quilt, then helped him pull off his riding boots. The captain kept his mouth tightly closed and bravely tried not to make a sound, although he was obviously in a great deal of pain.

"I'm done for, boys," he said once he was settled on the sofa.

The tiny parlor of the farmhouse was now crowded with soldiers. Their dusty boots scuffed the wood floor and sullied the fine carpet that had been carried here from Baltimore. They had their hats off and although they all wore beards that hid their expressions, she could see how sad their eyes looked. It was stifling in the parlor, and the small room quickly filled with the smell of sweat and dirty wool uniforms, horses, leather and blood. They could hardly move without tripping over each other's long cavalry sabers.

"We shall send for the doctor," Louisa said. "Samuel, you can walk into Lisbon." It was six miles away from Cooksville by way of the Baltimore Pike, but it was the closest physician and in the opposite direction from where the skirmish had taken place, just in case there were more milia in the woods.

As Samuel moved to go, Hollis shifted over to stop him.

"Ain't no sense going for a doctor," he said quietly. "He's gut shot, and there ain't a thing a doctor can do for him."

"He's right," said the captain, even though Hollis hadn't meant for him to overhear. "And that's a fact. Now you boys get out of here while you still can. I'll see you in heaven or I'll see you in hell, but I ain't goin' to see you caught by no Yankee patrol. That's an order."

One by one, the rugged soldiers mumbled their farewells and shuffled nosily from the room, making Louisa flinch as their swords banged against the furniture and doorway. Hollis was the last to go. He reached down and gripped the wounded man's bloody hands. He seemed to be working up something to say. "Captain—"

"Go on now, Hollis. And take care of yourself and the others. Somebody will have to get home from this damn war."

Hollis nodded. He had set his lips firmly, as if to keep any words from coming out. He nodded at Samuel and Louisa, then went out.

Moments later they heard the men ride off. Louisa looked out the back window and saw them moving down the hill. One of the men was leading the captain's horse by the reins, its saddle empty.

"There they go," the captain said. His head was turned toward the window, and Louisa realized that he was listening to the sounds of the riders moving away. "God bless them boys."

Samuel went out on the porch and was back in a moment. "They brought our mare back, at least," he reported. "She's tied to the railing."

"It's awful Christian of ya'll to let the boys leave me here," Captain Asher said. "I'm sorry we took your chickens. And I'm right sorry for bleeding all over your sofa, ma'am."

"Hush now," Louisa said. "You need your strength. Samuel, go fetch a glass of water and some towels."

"Louisa, the rebels are gone now. We don't have to—"

"Samuel, that's enough."

He seemed about to protest further, but thought better of it and went to get what she had asked for.

Louisa helped the captain sit up enough so that he could drink. The bullet hole made an ugly, gaping wound in his belly. More blood gushed out whenever he moved. Beneath the rebel's permanently tanned and weather-beaten face, the pallor of his skin had become quite pale.

"I am sorry to see you in this state, Captain."

"Dying ain't so hard," he said. "Living is harder these days."

"Just save your strength," Louisa urged him. He seemed awfully calm, but Louisa wasn't. She had seen her share of death from disease, but never before had she seen someone dying from a bullet wound. In her parlor, no less. Barely half an hour before, this soldier had been sitting tall in the saddle, an apparently invincible rebel cavalryman. Now he was in prostrate on the sofa, his blood steadily leaking out, too weak to move.

"Ain't no use pretending," he said. "I've seen wounds like this plenty of times. If the bullet had come out the back of me, I'd be dead already. With the bullet in my belly I won't last the day."

Samuel brought the water and towels. While the captain

drank from the glass, Louisa used a small towel to staunch the blood as best she could. She tried not to think about her towels and sofa being ruined because it wasn't Christian. She unbuttoned his uniform coat, but the calico shirt beneath was plastered to his skin with sweat and blood. He winced as she attempted to peel the shirt away to get at the wound. Louisa went about it clumsily because she was no nurse.

"Just leave it, ma'am. It's no use, anyhow. Just put a bandage on and let that be the end of it."

Louisa had reached the limit of her nursing skills and Samuel, watching from a few feet away, made no effort to help. For a man used to managing a railroad, he seemed incapable now of doing anything more than looking on with an expression of dumb helplessness. Not that she was surprised; she had found that most men were squeamish when it came to the sight of blood. There was almost the small fact that not so long ago, he had been ready to shoot the rebels himself. She put the bandage on as best she could and sat back.

"You're awful kind, ma'am," the captain said.

"Can we do anything for you, Captain?" she asked.

"Well, ma'am, if it ain't too much trouble, I would like to write a letter home if you all have some paper and a pencil handy."

Samuel brought some paper—all that they had on hand was some B&O Railroad stationery, but it would do. "Do you wish me to write it out for you?" Louisa asked.

"No, thank you, ma'am," the young captain said politely. "This will help take my mind off things."

He lay quietly on the sofa, propped up on a pillow, and wrote his letter home. Louisa would have sworn she could watch the color drain out of him in the way that the light faded from the sky in the evening. His bandages became sodden with blood. The only sound was the scratch of his pencil on paper. After a while, they heard the rattle of gunfire in the distance, much farther away than the skirmish in the woods had been.

"That will be down by the river," Samuel announced, listening with a practiced ear. The bridge where the Washington Road crossed the Patapsco River near Hoods Mill was two miles as the crow flew, and Samuel often listened for the B&O train crossing the road at that point, blowing its whistle and going about the business of the railroad.

"Sounds like things are pretty hot for the boys," Asher said. "They must have run into real soldiers, not like that militia we run into, although they did a right good job on me."

The sound of the firing in the distance brought a patrol of regular Union cavalry racing past the farmhouse, their horses in a lather in the summer heat. They must have been riding down every country lane, chasing every rumor of rebel cavalry. The Union cavalry was well-equipped, with gleaming saddle leather and fresh blue uniforms, so different from the near rags that the Confederates wore. Samuel and Louisa stepped out on the porch as they went by, and one of the riders reined his horse in long enough to shout, "Seen any Rebs?"

Louisa thought about the Confederate officer in her parlor. She glanced at Samuel, whose face was carefully blank, looking at the soldier. He was leaving it up to Louisa to reply.

"Down that road," Louisa answered, pointing in the direction where the other cavalrymen were rapidly disappearing in the direction of the barn and woods beyond. The rider touched the sides of his mount with his spurs and rode off.

She looked at Samuel. "Thank you," she said.

"Let the man go in peace," he said quietly. "Besides, I'd rather not try to explain to angry Union troops why we have a wounded Confederate in our care."

When they went back inside, the Confederate asked, his voice weak, "Were those Yankees?"

"Just passing by. Did you finish your letter?" Louisa asked, hoping to change the subject.

"Yes, ma'am. I mentioned in there how good you and your

husband was to me. My family's address is at the top, if you would be so kind as to see it delivered."

"Of course," Louisa said. She took the letter, handed it to Samuel. "Do you need anything?"

"Another drink of water would be good, ma'am. Just a drink of water, if it's no trouble." His voice was barely a whisper.

Louisa went to the kitchen to fetch the pitcher of water. When she returned to the parlor, Samuel looked at her and shook his head. "He's gone," he said.

There was a noise on the porch, and Samuel went to find one of the Crook boys there, sent by his mother to make sure everything was all right. In an excited tone, the boy explained how the Confederates had ridden right past their farm, not bothering to ransack it, for which his mother was grateful. The boy also brought news that rebel raiders had burned the bridge at Sykesville and torn up the train tracks.

Louisa said to Samuel, "The Crook boy can help you bury the soldier."

She had never prepared a body for burial, but there was not much to it. They emptied the soldier's pockets, finding more Confederate currency and a broken watch, then bundled these with the letter to send to his family. She got an old blanket and spread it on the floor. Samuel and the neighbor's boy lifted the body off the sofa and Louisa knelt to cross the arms on the chest. Thankfully, he had died with his eyes closed. She pulled the blanket up and around him, tucking and pinning it into a neat package. A coffin would have been nice, but there wasn't time for that. When she was finished, Samuel and the boy carried the body out and put it in the back of the wagon, hitched up to the mare left by the rebels. Louisa bundled up the bandages and the bloody quilt, which had managed to protect the sofa. With a guilty pang, she realized that she was glad her sofa had been spared.

Louisa waited an hour before marching across the field to join them. Samuel and the boy had dug a grave on a high ridge in the field, where several large white rocks thrust from the soil, making the ground unsuitable for crops. A few small butternut and locust trees had taken root among the rocks. It was a good spot for burying, windswept but peaceful, with the high ground offering fine views of the surrounding farmland. The body was already in the grave. Samuel said a prayer, and then he and the boy went to work with the shovels. Once they were done, Louisa picked some daisies and placed them atop the mound of fresh earth. Samuel thanked the boy and sent him home with a coin for his efforts.

She and Samuel stood together on the hilltop, side by side, watching the afternoon turn to a perfect summer evening. To the northeast, a pall of smoke rose from what must have been the burning bridge across the Patapsco, but it was too far away to concern them. So much had happened since morning that the day had an overstuffed quality like a sack filled to bursting, as if too much had been forced into the narrow span of hours. The dashing Confederate captain was truly a gray ghost now. There was no way Louisa could know it, but in years to come the road to the farm would be abandoned and mostly forgotten, except for the occasional hunters and farmers who traveled it and sometimes saw a silent gray rider on the road.

"What a day this has been, Samuel," Louisa said. "Confederate soldiers raided us, fought a skirmish on our land, and one of them died in our parlor." Saying this aloud did not make it sound any more real.

"Yes," he answered.

She glanced at him, standing with the shovel in his hands, looking down at the grave. Handsome as always, with the evening breeze ruffling his hair. She shuddered and took his arm, thinking how easily it could have been Samuel in that grave, or in a grave someplace far away and forgotten as this field. She was ashamed of herself for thinking him a coward. Her opinion of war had changed considerably since that morning.

"Samuel, when we go back to Baltimore, I do not wish you to enlist."

"Louisa—"

"Promise me you won't, Samuel."

"I won't enlist," he said. After a moment he added ruefully, "Besides, there will be plenty enough to do repairing all the damage to the railroad that these Confederates have done."

She hugged him. Then Samuel took the mare's bridle, and Louisa and her husband walked slowly back across the field toward the farmhouse. Only once did Louisa look back, and in the evening light the fresh earth of the grave looked like a wound in the green fields all around it.

ESSAYS

Covered bridge at Fair Hill, Maryland

NOVEL RUN: REFLECTIONS ON WRITING AND RUNNING

B ecause I'm a writer and a runner, I've often noticed that setting pen to paper is a lot like setting foot to pavement. Both take will power and the ability to go the distance. Writers and runners enjoy a challenge, something to test their limits, like finding a good metaphor or tackling a five-mile run.

Considering that writers turn to the same inner place as runners, it's surprising that there are no great novels about running. Whole shelves are filled with novels about baseball and fishing and even football. There aren't any writers who are famous for their running. Maybe running isn't glamorous enough. Or maybe it's not possible to fully capture the intangibles of running?

That's too bad, because running can open up the senses as much as the pores, especially during those runs away from the blacktop. In my head, I try to compose descriptions of leaves crackling under my running shoes or the squish-squelch of wet grass. On my laptop computer, however, the words get all tied up in double knots.

For those who have felt it, a good run builds like a good story. Those first strides as I find my rhythm are like the opening lines of a novel: It is a crisp autumn evening when I set out on my run, heading for the trails along the Chesapeake and Delaware Canal. (PROLOGUE.)

Cold wind rubs like sandpaper across my puffing cheeks. (RISING ACTION)

I come to a hill, pumping my arms and leaning into the grade. Halfway up, a cramp gnaws at my side. (CONFLICT)

Then I coast down the hill, the cramp gone, the cool air smelling of leaves and so rich my lungs can't get enough. (THE DENOUEMENT)

Back at the edge of town, the wild land gives way to yards and gardens. I sprint the final few hundred feet to the house, energized by that fall air. The water is blue as a vein and the sky is turning cobalt as I coast to a stop. (EPILOGUE)

That final sprint felt great. After all, most runners, like most writers, enjoy a good ending.

ORIGINALLY PUBLISHED IN *RUNNING TIMES*, December 2001.

WRITER'S CHOICE: WILLIAM STYRON, WHITE WINE, AND THE POWER OF IMAGINATION

Tall, white-haired, and with a Virginia gentleman's accent, William Styron looked and sounded like a Southern writer. But what impressed me was that we had the same taste in alcoholic beverages.

This was in 1986. I was nineteen and the Pulitzer Prize-winning author was visiting Washington College in Chestertown, Maryland, to instruct and inspire the young writers there, which is why I found myself at the door of the President's House to have dinner with Styron, faculty, and students.

A solemn-faced waiter wearing a white jacket greeted me just inside the door of the 18th-century mansion.

"May I get you a cocktail?" he asked.

Under the circumstances, it felt more like a pop quiz than a question. It didn't seem likely that the bar at the president's house was stocked with National Bohemian beer.

"Ahh . . . I'll have a glass of white wine," I said.

I heard a deep voice behind me. The great man himself was coming in the door. "That sounds like a fine idea," Styron told the waiter. "I'll have the same."

At that point, I stammered something witty like, "Hello, Mr. Styron," and retreated—glass of wine in hand—into the crowded house. I hadn't read any of his books yet and feared that he might ask me how I liked them. The college had invited prospective freshmen to the event, and they were there with their parents, getting a feel for the place. Several parents looked uncomfortable in that genteel Tidewater setting, or maybe it was only the thought of the tuition that was making them sweat.

"What wonderful knickknacks," one nervous mother remarked to Libby Cater, wife of College President Douglas Cater and lady of the house.

Libby, ever so polite, replied, "Oh, do you like my jade collection?"

As the newly educated mother and daughter moved on, Libby turned to me and confided how pleased she was that Styron, a one-time neighbor of the Caters, was visiting the college. Then her voice dropped a note as she added, "You know, one day he was out getting his mail when I was in the yard and he showed me a royalty check for forty thousand dollars." Libby appreciated good writing, but she also knew the value of all things green.

Over dinner, Styron shared how the idea for *Sophie's Choice* was born in a flash of inspiration that soon had him on a research trip to a concentration camp. Published in 1979, *Sophie's Choice* became a bestseller and was made into a film starring Meryl Streep as the pale Holocaust survivor. Styron graciously answered the students' questions on writing. He was self-effacing, even subdued, which makes sense now: this was soon after he nearly committed suicide, as revealed in his memoir, *Darkness Visible: A Memoir of Madness*. One thing became clear, which was that Styron was a thoughtful man who loved storytelling and the craft of writing.

He read that evening from a work in progress about his days as a Marine during World War II, tough material for a college-age audience forty years removed from their grandfathers' war. However, that didn't stop me from later reading *Lie Down in Darkness*, an experimental 1951 novel with echoes of Faulkner that nonetheless seemed as relevant to the '80s as two other hot novels of self-destruction I devoured about the same time, *Less Than Zero* and *Bright Lights, Big City*.

Late at night, I would plow through all sorts of books that had nothing to do with class assignments. On a Styron kick now, and hoping I might be able to pair his advice to something I found in his writing, I read *Sophie's Choice*. The true horror of Sophie's situation wouldn't sink in until I dipped into the novel again after having children of my own. Now, from a parent's perspective, Sophie's guilt and grief seem unbearable. The novel's language is lush as a steamy Southern night. This is writing that takes its time covering more than 600 pages.

The book I never got around to was *The Confessions of Nat Turner*, about a bloody slave revolt in 1831. Since I seem to have made a habit of catching up on Styron after the man has come and gone, I'll have to read that one next.

Even if I'll never write like Styron, I understand from him that it is the writer's imagination that matters most of all. You don't have to be a Polish Jew or an African-American slave to understand your characters. A good writer must be able to imagine his way into his characters' souls.

"A great book should leave you with many experiences, and slightly exhausted," Styron once said. "You should live several lives while reading it."

I won't say that Styron inspired me to be a writer, but he certainly taught me that it was OK to be one. . . and that a glass of white wine was a perfectly acceptable cocktail.

THIS ESSAY WAS PREVIOUSLY PUBLISHED by Scripps Howard News Service, 2006.

THE ACCIDENTAL LIBRARIAN

L anding a job at the library was serendipitous for me as a
  local author because I had already spent many hours
researching there. Suddenly, I found myself on the opposite side
of the reference desk.

There was a learning curve in stamping those due dates,
finding the location of the nearest AA meeting, looking up the
title of the third book in Laurell K. Hamilton's new series, or
cutting out paper fish for a children's program—all at the same
time. For a librarian, even a part-time one, juggling lots of tasks
comes with the territory.

For me, working at the library has been an eye-opener about
the way that libraries provide front-line public service to a popu-
lation that is often vulnerable or unempowered—the unem-
ployed or impoverished, the not-so-tech savvy, the very young or
very old, and the homeless.

On my first night working the reference desk, a young homeless woman wandered in, dressed completely in hot pink from
her puffy ski jacket to her mittens and moon boots. Cold air
washed in behind her as the automatic doors whisked open and
closed. It was a real January bonecracker, down in the single
digits.

Obviously, this young person was in distress. There were some language barriers as well, but the librarians worked out that she needed a warm place to stay. I called around to the local homeless shelters but was told they were full on that frigid night.

I soon found that librarians are reluctant to take "no" for an answer. My colleagues jumped in and called churches, the police station, halfway houses. The responses were: *sorry, can't help, full.* As we neared closing time, our pink lady opted to push on to the next town. The staff offered to chip in and put her up in a motel, but when she declined, they used their own money to arrange a taxi so that she wouldn't have to walk those wintry miles. It wasn't the best ending, but she had found a place to warm up and someone to advocate for her before she moved on.

I've learned that the library attracts people from all walks of life. Coming through the doors are patrons who drive new cars and some who can't afford a car, students researching projects, seniors who spend their days reading newspapers, teens who furtively check out steam punk vampire novels—and each other. Even in the age of Google, patrons pepper the reference desk with every question imaginable.

Librarians spend a lot of time helping middle-aged job seekers, often because these patrons lack computer skills. They've been set adrift by layoffs in a new world where looking for a job means clicking through online applications like some kind of lab rat. The Great Recession never really ended for them. When I stopped seeing "a regular," I could only hope it meant that he or she had found a job.

Another quirk of library life is that several branches provide an unsung public service for the middle school age group. When school lets out, some libraries morph into something more like the set of a Nickelodeon sitcom. These kids are too old for day care, too young to be home alone, and so the library provides a kind of informal after-school care. Sometimes the library closes, the parents are late, and the kids have to wait outside. One of the librarians usually sits in her car out in the parking lot until the last kid gets picked up.

Ultimately, I've discovered from my time working the reference desk that a library is mostly about people trying to move forward one book, one reference question, one online job application at a time. It is an institution that has evolved to reflect the digital age in which we live without ever forgetting its role in serving the public.

"LIFE LESSONS AT THE LIBRARY" was previously published as an op-ed article in *The Baltimore Sun*, May 2019

SNAPSHOT: THE DAY NIXON RESIGNED—AUGUST 9, 1974

"Come in, kids, you have to see this."

My friend Stephen Johnston and I were playing in the foundation of the summer porch my dad was building. It made a great fort. The fact that dad was making it out of scrap lumber and windows salvaged from a demolished school, now stacked in tottering heaps, added to the war zone effect.

"Quick! Hurry up! It's on television right now!"

Steve and I really didn't want to pause in battling the Nazis or maybe it was the Indians (this being a politically incorrect era) but in we went.

My mother remains a great believer in witnessing momentous events. She had her own—watching the Beatles on *The Ed Sullivan Show*, or standing in the bitter cold to catch a glimpse of John F. Kennedy.

She wanted us kids to have our own memories of momentous events. "We're going to the Bicentennial parade!" "I know it's two o'clock in the morning but you have to see Haley's Comet!" "Come quick, your father is trimming the trees over the house with his shotgun!"

That last one sent me running. But watching something on TV, not so much.

The black-and-white Zenith television complete with a "rabbit ears" antennae and the sofa set from Montgomery Ward were about the only modern touches in our Civil War-era farmhouse.

Sweaty and impatient, Steve and I gathered around the TV where we usually watched *Emergency!* or *The Waltons* ... or *The Battle of the Bulge* if we were lucky. On live television, President Nixon crossed the White House lawn and boarded a huge helicopter. He paused on the steps to flash a V sign, making him look a bit like Spock. Then he flew away.

"You boys will remember this," mom said. "It's not every day that the president resigns."

We drank cherry Kool-Aid and ate bologna sandwiches on Wonderbread, then went back to playing war. It was a steamy Maryland summer day, with a hazy overcast, but it was cool among the concrete blocks and foundation ditches.

Maybe it was important to see Nixon walk out of the White House on live television. But in some ways it was more memorable to have in my mind a perfect snapshot of being seven years old on a particular day—noon on August 9, 1974. Momentous, indeed.

ORIGINALLY PUBLISHED IN *CAPSTONE*, Summer 2014.

BORN IN A GREENHOUSE

One of my favorite memories is of my father working in his greenhouse on a February night, his strong fingers transplanting delicate petunia seedlings, and me keeping him company as I read a frontier adventure novel called *Winter Danger* by William O. Steele.

I'm about eight years old. There's old-school country music on the radio, turned up loud enough to drown out the ripple of greenhouse plastic in the winter wind. The only light is from a fluorescent tube suspended overhead. We both strain to see as my eyes follow the words and my father's fingers untangle the seedlings' roots.

I don't come from a gardening family—but from a greenhouse family. Since 1970, my parents have been in the business of supplying stores and gardeners with pots and packs of flower and vegetable starts.

Things have come a long way from the days when my mother seeded all the trays of tomatoes, herbs, and flowers at the kitchen table at night, then set them in a sunny picture window to germinate. Back then my father would transplant the sprouted seedlings into pots and market packs in their home-made greenhouse, a greenhouse carved from the cornfields surrounding their Civil War-era farmhouse. Now my parents have employees and delivery trucks and enough greenhouses to cover an acre with plastic.

February was always my favorite month in the greenhouses. I'm reminded of this on a recent visit to my parents' farm. A rare Maryland blizzard has piled two feet of snow outside and the white blanket has lingered in the bitter cold. Inside a greenhouse, however, the warm, humid air is the very breath of spring. My father is giving me a tour. I carry my own son, one-year old Aidan, and we wander from greenhouse to greenhouse.

Dad offers lessons and tips about the various plants, just like in the old days growing up. "What three things does it take for a plant to grow?" he once asked me. I pointed to a sack of fertilizer. "Nitrogen, phosphorus, and potassium?" I said. "No, David. Nutrients, water, and sunshine." All these years later, we pass a sack of fertilizer, and I almost expect to hear his question.

Looking at the snow outside, I'm reminded of another long-ago February snowstorm. This one came at night and dumped two feet of heavy, wet snow in a few hours. My father was at his outside job—snow removal for a governmental complex, of all things—so my mother and two brothers and I were left to save the greenhouses. We worked all night with long-handled brooms to clear off the snow, but it was a losing battle. My mother cried as the heavy snow finally crushed the frames, tiny plants, and my parents' hopes. By then it was 2:00 a.m. As the snow piled even deeper on the broken frames, there was nothing more we could do but go to bed. I was 11 years old and staggering with exhaustion.

Anyone who has been part of a family business knows the blood and sweat and tears involved. The plant business isn't any different. It's not a hobby; it's a livelihood. There were a lot of times when we all worked late into the night, filling orders by flashlight, the greenhouses dark and lush as a jungle. I never had to get an after-school job because there was always more than enough work to do at home filling pots, transplanting, shipping orders, tending plants.

Money was not the only motivating factor. My father loves plants. He can talk about plants for hours, driving all but the most diehard gardener to seek escape. He always tried to share that love with us.

What's strange is that my father is about the last person anyone would have put money on to become a horticulturist. He grew up helping tend his own father's bar in Boston. Healey's Bar was a shot-and-a-beer joint where the cigarette smoke was thick and the Narragansett Ale flowed freely. But my father had a longing for blue sky and green things—his mother had a fit once when she caught him sterilizing potting soil in her oven. He has told me how he almost took over his father's bar—but was always glad he chose plants instead. After getting a degree in horticulture from the University of Connecticut, he and my mother bought a farm in Maryland, two displaced Yankees tucked below the Mason-Dixon Line.

He's a plant man, through and through. He grabs up a handful of soil from a pot and lets it sift through his fingers, measuring the heft and potential of it.

Why do we become what we become, different from or the same as the parents who raised us? All I know is that our paths were revealed that February night so many years ago, when we worked side by side, my father bent over his plants, my own head bent over a book. It's a moment that stands frozen in time, as some childhood memories do. Both of us were doing what we loved best. And that's all that any of us can hope to do, if we want to live our lives without regret.

ORIGINALLY PUBLISHED in *Green Prints* magazine, Winter 2000-01.

TRAPLINE

When I was a kid I had an after-school job that was a little out of the ordinary, but when you grow up on a farm it means that the usual employment options such as flipping burgers or stocking shelves aren't readily available. At eleven, I was too young for those jobs, anyhow. There were some old traps in the barn, so I oiled them up and headed into the woods, intent on being a trapper.

In hindsight, the concept of trapping animals seems terribly cruel; it's lucky for my conscience and the local fur-bearers that I never actually caught anything. It's even luckier that I didn't lose any fingers. Mainly, the trapline was an excuse for getting out into the woods alone and maybe skipping a few farm chores. After being in school all day, there was nothing better than trekking through the fields and among the trees, especially in winter. I would scramble out of my school clothes and into battered jeans, boots, and an Army hat from the Korean War that I bought at Sunny's Surplus for a couple of bucks.

I always carried my rifle, an ancient single-shot .22. The stock was battered and scarred as an ax handle. The back sight was permanently bent, which made a good excuse for not being able to shoot straight.

Wandering the woods was like being in some vast abandoned mansion. The bare tree branches formed the roof, the various deer paths were hallways; the clearings were like ballrooms. There was the hushed quiet of a library, disturbed only by the creek that burbled over a rocky bottom. Crystalline sheets of ice formed across the deep places. There was one spot where a massive fallen log crossed the creek and I would use that as a bridge, crossing effortlessly across the snow-covered trunk.

Once or twice a voice startled me, and I would be surprised that I had spoken my thoughts out loud. I was like one of those Old West trappers, driven mad by solitude.

I knew about trappers from reading frontier adventure novels by William O. Steele, real Cowboys and Indians stuff that's long since out of fashion. This was when flintlocks and buckskin and Daniel Boone were just giving way to light sabers and Luke Skywalker and The Force.

In a real woods, not a well-tended state park or a groomed trail but a place that is seldom visited by people, you see and hear things that others rarely witness.

One time I saw a coyote stricken with mange so that it was hairless, a horror that some call a Chupacabra. The creature hopped off into the woods before I could even think to move, my heart pounding.

The land has other mysteries. That January, I found a stone arrowhead along the creek bank. My imagination wandered. What long-ago hunter had shot that arrow? At the edge of a field was an old dump from the days when there was no such thing as the county landfill. Rusty cans and abandoned whiskey bottles sprouted from the dead leaves. That hard-drinking farmer, long gone, sometimes left a splash of amber liquid that swished around the bottom of the bottle. Curious, I unscrewed the top. That stale whiskey smelled like adulthood.

Another time I discovered a bleached deer skull with a single pellet of buckshot embedded in the bone. The one thing I never found, but always wished for, was a relic from the Civil War skirmish fought nearby. I was always envious of the old man next door who dug up a Confederate belt buckle during spring plowing.

Away from the creek, I could hear trees rasping overhead in the cold. If you don't believe in spirits, just listen to the trees in the winter wind. Spirits, memories, call it what you will—there is something riding on the wind. It's like listening to a foreign language, knowing the sounds have meanings that you can't quite decipher, but you can understand the tone. The wind sounded lonesome and mournful, with a whisper of threat.

There is a poem by James Dickey that comes close to that feeling, "In the Mountain Tent." Dickey wrote, *Through the thought-out leaves of the wood/Into the minds of animals.* The poet seems to hint that the woods and creatures inhabiting wild places do think, possibly on a frequency beyond the range of human understanding.

Late that winter, someone stole all my traps. They were just gone. My dad and I formed a posse to track down the culprit. We had a suspect, because the farmer on the next property over often went raccoon hunting at night. We could hear the high, lonesome sound of his dogs baying at midnight through the woods. The dogs ignored property lines and fences, and so did the hunter. Sure enough, tracks in the snow led toward his farm. We got in the pickup and drove there. The traps were piled up on a concrete pad by the water pump out in front of the farmhouse.

All those hunting dogs announced our arrival. The farmer came out and shifted from foot to foot, looking from the traps, to us, then back again, figuring how to play it.

"I thought someone was poachin' on your land," he said. It wasn't really an explanation for why the farmer had trespassed and taken the traps in the first place.

"No, those belong to my son here," my father said calmly. "We'll take them back now."

We loaded the traps in the back of the truck. I can't

remember setting them again, and maybe I never did, but I'll always remember my dad standing in front of that farmhouse, showing me to stand up for what was yours.

With his bad knees, my father would have a hard time navigating the woods now, let alone tracking anyone through the snow. I'm older now than he was then, and I would seriously think twice, maybe three times, about crossing a creek on a snow-covered fallen log. My daughter worked in an ice cream shop and my own son is more interested in video games and less cruel after-school jobs, like working as a busboy. And I think that's just fine. We all leave our own tracks; we all find our own way.

Eventually I hung up the traps for good in the barn and moved on to other things like cars, sports, an after-school job in the family greenhouse business, and high school. The farm next door was sold off, the hunter's house was bulldozed, and the land is now covered in McMansions. The family farm remains like an island in suburbia. You certainly won't hear a hound hunting at night anymore; that's an echo from the past. The creek, however, is still there, running over rocks and through the woods, having a conversation with itself, flowing like the years themselves.

Recently, I visited the barn and saw the traps hanging from a nail. They were cold to the touch, rusted shut, like a closed chapter from a long time ago.

REFERENCE

Dickey, J. (1978). *Poems 1957-1967*. Middletown, CT: Wesleyan University Press.

ORIGINALLY PUBLISHED IN *CAPSTONE*, Winter 2015.

MEMORIAL DAY: MEDALS & MEMORIES OF WORLD WAR II

E very Memorial Day, my grandfather would make a trip to his summer cottage to cut the grass and put the picnic table in the backyard.

Although he was a veteran, he wasn't much on parades or hanging out flags. He tended to smile at such things, although those who didn't know him might have mistaken it for a sneer. One side of his thin mouth would twist the wrong way, at odds with the rest of his face.

The Second World War had left him with that crooked smile. He had manned an antiaircraft gun aboard the *USS Leo* in the Pacific and the concussion of the gun had damaged his facial nerves. It wasn't much of a wound, considering what had happened to some veterans. And it certainly wasn't his life, which 400,000 Americans lost during the war.

But the damage went much deeper than the muscles of his face. Forty years after the war, I'd hear the pain in his voice as he told me about what he had seen and done in the Pacific. Then there was the son—my father—born while he was off fighting and who knew his father only as a stranger.

If Frank Healey were still alive at this 75th year after the war, I think he would have greeted the commemorations with that bent smile. If anyone had asked, he might even have told them what the war had been like for a sailor from Boston.

A RED SOX game was on the radio, turned down low, as grandad and I saw on the front porch of his house in Watertown, on the outskirts of Boston. The summer evening was giving way to a dusky twilight. A good time for stories.

"They used to call me 'Pops' because I was 34 years old. Thirty four! Most of those guys was 19, 20. I was the oldest one on board. I think I was older than the captain."

Across the street, a young man stepped out of a grinder shop, threw the sandwich wrapper on the ground, and kept walking.

Grandad jumped up from his chair, the sports pages in one hand and a can of beer in the other.

"Hey you!" he yelled. "What the hell do you think you're doin'? Pick that up, for crissake."

The offender stopped, grabbed up the paper, and scurried away.

"You told him," I said, with all the admiration of a 12-year-old.

"What's he think he's doin', throwin' his trash in the street?" His damaged face was twisted in a snarl. "Don't ever let me catch you doin' that."

Heck, after that, I didn't so much as leave an empty soda bottle on the dining room table.

FRANK HEALEY HAD COME from another era, one we look back at today and see as an America still fresh and new and a little innocent, yet somehow worn out when you see the old black-and-white photos of the hard-drinking laborers that were the Boston Irish.

Both his parents were immigrants of Irish descent. He dropped out of school after the eighth grade to go to work. During the Depression, he shared a job with two other young men and spent the rest of his time playing baseball. He never missed Mass on Sundays. On a pleasure cruise in Boston Harbor one weekend he met a nice Irish girl, Mary O'Connell, who became his wife.

In a shoebox full of photographs that serves as my grandmother's family archive, a snapshot taken in the Pacific of gunner Frank Healey posing with his Navy buddies shows a somewhat paunchy man with a craggy face, definitely no boy in a sailor suit. He looks like a teacher on a field trip with a class of high school kids. Some of those boys from his gun crew never came home.

The war stories would come later. When he got back to Boston, life picked up where it had left off. Everybody's goal in those days when the immigrant ethic was still fresh was for their children to be better off than their parents had been.

My grandfather opened Healey's Bar and ran it for 20 years. The family moved out of a crowded apartment and into their own home. To escape the city's summer heat, my grandparents built a cottage near the beach on Boston's South Shore. Their three children went to college. There were Red Sox games, grandchildren, friends down at the Eagles. Nobody talked much about the war. Anyhow, there were new wars in Korea and Vietnam that younger men were going off to fight. Like many World War II veterans, my grandfather never made it to this 75th commemoration season, or even to the 50th. He smoked a lot of cigarettes tending bar, and he died of throat cancer in the summer of 1986.

One evening, the year before he died, he and I were sitting outside the beach cottage he had built years ago for his young family. Lately, he had been talking a lot about the war. I think he knew he didn't have much time left because there was something a little urgent in his stories, like he had to pass them on, like he had to let us know. Sometimes, too, it was as if he were just talking out loud, trying to puzzle out something in his own mind. Maybe, after all those years, he was trying to figure out why he was still there, talking with his grandson, when so many others had not returned.

Night was coming on, but a few bees still hummed in the rhododendron blooms nearby as he worked his thumb through the sweat on his cold can of Budweiser. He started telling me about one of the fights he'd seen.

"Some of the things that happened. Jesus. I remember there was this suicide plane—a kamikaze—coming right for us."

He sipped his beer, described the Zero strafing the deck as it came in. "This Zero was heading right for the ship and all I could do was fire at it." He put his hands close together, gripping an imaginary gun and squinting up at a Japanese Zero he'd shot out of the sky 40 years ago.

"Boom. Boom. Boom. The crazy son-of-a-bitch kept coming. Then the plane tilted up on its side" —one hand showed the angle of the crashing Zero— "and went into the ocean. The gun stopped firing and I looked around to see what was wrong." He sniffed, sipped his beer. "The guys in my gun crew were all dead. I'd been talking to them just a minute ago."

It's hard to know what to do when you're a kid and your grandfather is crying. I wish now that I had put a hand on his shoulder, told him it was all right. Instead, I looked away and slapped at the mosquitoes.

"Jesus, they're going to eat us alive," he finally said, as if nothing had happened. "You go on inside. I'll be along in a minute."

A couple of days later, my grandfather gave me his campaign ribbons, those bright bars worn on a uniform. They represented the American Campaign Medal, Asiatic—Pacific Campaign Medal with two bronze stars, World War II Victory Medal with one bronze star. He knew exactly where the ribbons were when we went upstairs to get them. There was no peering in closets or rummaging in the attic. He opened a drawer and took them out.

"Are you sure?" I asked. After all, these were his war medals. Prized possessions.

"I want you to have them," he said.

Like my grandfather, I also keep them in a certain place. I take them out from time to time to think about "Pops" and his time aboard the *USS Leo*. As I write this, they're on my computer keyboard, a strip of once—colorful ribbons now faded by time.

Along with the ribbons, he also passed along what I know now was a simple prayer. "I hope you kids never have to go through that," he said. He wasn't talking about the Depression or running a shot-and-a-beer joint or dying of cancer. He meant the war.

I'm sure he would have liked to be here this Memorial Day. He'd be opening the cottage, cutting the grass. I'd introduce him to his great-grandchildren. If he told his war stories again, this time, I'd touch his shoulder. This time, I'd tell him it was all right. This time, I would thank him.

"MEDALS AND MEMORIES OF WWII" was originally published in the *Cecil Whig* newspaper on Memorial Day, 1994.

VACATION DREAMING

S leet pelts against the windowpane as I thumb through one
of those glossy regional magazines, the kind with the slick
pages that are cold to the touch on a winter's night. The last
thing I want to read is another article about antiquing or the
best place to buy a crab cake. But I keep flipping pages, drawn to
the ads for art galleries and vacation homes that make me feel
like I'm visiting my own tiny printed square of sun-soaked real
estate.

All of a sudden, that's not a car I hear churning through the
slush outside—it's the sound of surf on a rocky beach. Dimly, it
registers that my favorite leather chair feels chilly and the living
room curtains are dancing in the draft. But I'm long gone by
then, having crossed some mental portal into the middle of
August.

One painting in particular grabs my attention. It shows an
old farmhouse rendered in grays and browns, in stark contrast to
the surrounding summer grass and the distant blur of trees.
There's a lean-to-addition like the one attached to the farmhouse where I grew up. There's usually a mudroom in there, or a
kitchen or a bathroom, added as a kind of afterthought, a
concession to modern times back in 1920. The painting tells a

story of hard winters and hot summers, of too little paint and too much weather. Smells seem to come right off the page: pine needles, salt air, and the musky damp rot of wood. The painting was so much like a snapshot out of time, so evocative of place and atmosphere that I didn't want it on my wall so much as I wanted to step into the scene itself, to visit that old house, maybe even live in it— at least for a week or two.

We've all known houses like this one, caught glimpses of them while exploring country roads on vacation. Artists are always putting them on canvas, recreating quaint scenes of cottages and summerhouses. The gallery ads in my magazine offer pages of a painting style that one might call the School of Summer Yearning. The landscape painting of the rustic house has become a genre all its own.

And yet, few of us would actually want to live in such a house. These are strictly vacation houses for that precious week or two of the year when we trade our wingtips for sandals, our suits for shorts. That week when there's nothing more pressing on the agenda than a daily swim, a good book, and a dinner of lobster or steamed crabs, depending upon your geography. Under these circumstances, a house with a lean-to-addition is well suited to be a temporary home in Maine or the Chesapeake Bay country.

Motivated by something like a childhood memory or wandering thoughts during Monday morning's staff meeting, we call up the real estate agent and reserve our week.

How quickly, though, reality sets in once we arrive months later. Cracked acorn shells on the kitchen counter indicate that a squirrel has been taking his meals there. The plaster ceiling in the hallway sags where the rain is getting in. There's peeling lead paint on the windowsills, knob-and-tube electrical wiring last updated during the Roosevelt administration. On Tuesday, we have to venture into the cellar to change a fuse because someone turned on the coffee pot and the toaster at the same time. By Wednesday, we've figured out how to get the toilet to flush properly by jiggling the handle three times. Lighting the old propane stove to boil a lobster requires a long match and the kind of courage that comes from a few glasses of wine. By Saturday we're glad to return home, if a bit winsomely, to that tract house with the big mortgage in Fox Chase Estates. Memories of our idyllic old house wear thin over time.

But it would be a mistake to rent something better. My own family did this once, settling into a nicely renovated vacation home owned by a doctor from Boston. There were new cabinets, cable TV, a deck that overlooked the salt marsh. It seemed like pretty nice digs until we visited some friends up the road who had rented a ramshackle old mansion with brown wallpaper that smelled of mildew, high ceilings, and lampshades with dusty tassels. The lamps themselves had brittle wires with round plugs and the light "switches" had buttons. We returned late to our upscale digs, marveling at the smell of new carpet and the digital clock on the microwave that read 12:03 a.m. Our friends paid less, and got the better house. Even now, it's their place that we still talk about.

A week or two away each summer is enough to last me until sometime after Christmas, when the ritual begins again. I start flipping through the magazines that have stacked up since August. I clip out gallery ads for those old house paintings along with photos of waterfront real estate and thumbtack them to the wall of my cramped office. The fluorescent light beats down, reminding me of how pale I've become. Whenever I glance at the pictures on the wall, I can almost smell the sunscreen. Somewhere in my mind a screen door slams.

Time to start vacation dreaming all over again.

ORIGINALLY PUBLISHED IN *DELMARVA QUARTERLY*, Winter 2008.

HEIRLOOM TOMATOES

There's nothing quite like a homegrown tomato. Luscious, juicy, red, still warm from the sun. They're even too good to waste on a sandwich. Better to slice them thick, sprinkle on a bit of salt, and call it lunch.

Just like a good wine connoisseur enjoys his Merlot or Beaujolais, I get pretty serious about my tomato varieties. There are the old standards like Rutgers or Better Boy you can get at a garden center, but they take second place to that heirloom Brandywine ripening nearby. It's like the difference between a wine with a screw top and one with a cork.

Something about these old varieties fascinates me. It's probably because we live in such a cookie-cutter world of strip malls and mass production where individuality is defined by which Internet Service Provider you subscribe to or your cell phone-calling plan. Heirloom tomatoes are by their very nature the opposite of mass-produced. They put us in touch not only with the earth of our gardens but with history. Each has a story to tell and a personality. They spark the gardener's imagination. There will always be those high-falutin' gardeners who cultivate antique roses, or even orchids, but tomatoes are far more interesting, not to mention practical. At least you can eat them.

This spring I'll be growing an Abe Lincoln tomato. I've been searching for a General Lee variety to give our garden some political balance. Maybe I'll plant the Lincoln and Lee tomatoes in Northern and Southern exposures, respectively, where they can keep an eye on each other. I imagine the Lincoln will be tall and gangly, full of rhetoric and always emancipating his tomatoes. Lee will be stately but resilient, surrendering to the frost long after all the others.

It is unlikely that General Lee himself enjoyed tomatoes. As a general rule, Civil War soldiers avoided tomatoes because many 19th-century folks believed these fruits of the nightshade family to be poisonous. (However, it's notable that General Lee traveled with caged laying hens so that he would always have fresh eggs.) Most soldiers lived mainly on salt pork and beans washed down with coffee, a meal that would have been much improved by a few hearty slices of tomato foraged from some Yankee's garden.

You'll notice that many heirloom tomatoes have a distinctly Southern heritage, probably because summer has to be long enough to grow a good tomato. Southerners, too, like a good story and a good name in a tomato. As the Southern writer Walker Percy said, "A good title should be like a good metaphor; it should intrigue without being too baffling or too obvious."

Which brings me back to Brandywine, on heirloom variety named for the Brandywine River in Pennsylvania. This name alone conjures images of Andrew Wyeth paintings for me—and the Revolutionary War battlefield where George Washington lost to the Redcoats. We've never actually bought Brandywine seeds because every Spring I depend on my old fishing buddy, Scott Lawrence, saving me a few from the seedlings he sprouts in his kitchen window. (Scott's tomatoes always turn out better—I suspect it's due to all those fish parts buried in his garden over the years.)

Growing up, we could count on a friend of my father's stopping by the farm to bring us a few seeds of what he called "Tennessee tomatoes." The man's name was actually Daniel Boone—

he was a distant relation to the pioneer—and this was an old variety his family grew on their farm back home in Tennessee. The ripe fruits were sweet and huge as melons, one slice filling a paper plate at picnics.

Another favorite in our yard is Longkeeper. These tomatoes are harvested late in the season. They're kind of hard and mealy for summer eating, but they live up to their name. We wrap them in newspaper and stow them some place cool. Then, at Thanksgiving or even for Christmas dinner, we slice homegrown tomatoes to grace the table.

Finally, there's Mortgage Lifter. I love the name of this tomato. Legend says this variety was created by a man named M.C. Byles or "Radiator Charlie" back in the 1930s. He must have been quite a character. The story goes that Charlie opened a radiator repair shop at the foot of a steep hill and picked up a lot of business from trucks that didn't make it to the top. Also, he developed this variety of hefty tomatoes, selling so many plants for $1 apiece that he paid off his $6,000 mortgage in six years.

For most of us, lifting the mortgage is going to take more than selling tomato plants by the side of the road, but you've got to admire Charlie's spirit. I planted a few in what used to be a flowerbed alongside the house. If nothing else, we saved on our grocery bill.

I like the idea of vegetables with history, even if some of those histories sound like tall tales. After all, a tomato that tastes good is a delight, but a tomato that tastes good and tells a story is like having an old friend to dinner.

ORIGINALLY PUBLISHED IN *DELMARVA QUARTERLY*, Summer 2004.

LIFE'S RICH COMPOST

My wife had a hard time selling me on the need for a compost pile.

"It's going to smell," I argued, imagining rotting potato peels and vegetable scraps turning to mush. "There's no room for a compost pile."

"We'll see," said my wife.

And we did. The compost pile went right next to the garden shed. The result was no raggedy backyard heap of grass clippings and brush, but a neat, four-sided box. The scraps to build it were left over from a friend's new deck. It's about three feet high and three feet square, with gaps between the boards to let in air. The boards on one side slide out to expose the whole pile for mixing and removing the compost.

That was years ago, and since then seemingly countless buckets of rich, black compost have been mixed into the soil of our flower beds and vegetable garden boxes. The result has been towering stands of white-blooming Phlox David by the front porch, a Magnolia grandiflora that has grown tall enough to obscure the neighbors' house from the kitchen window, and meaty Brandywine tomatoes the size of softballs.

Going around and spreading the compost is a good way to

remind ourselves of the story that goes with each plant. My wife bought the phlox simply because it had my name, David—long before I became "Daddy" or just "Honey." The magnolia came from a spring plant sale at the University of Delaware horticulture department. The tomato seedlings arrive each spring from a friend's kitchen window.

If gardening is a hobby, composting can became an obsession. When my wife and I cook, we have a compulsive need to save all the vegetable scraps for the compost pile. These all go into a green plastic container with a tight-fitting lid that sits beside the kitchen sink, awaiting transfer to the compost pile outside. It quickly fills up with stumps of broccoli too tough for the stir-fry, the carrot tops that didn't make it into the pot of chicken soup, the snapped-off ends of asparagus.

My wife and I have a competition going to out-do each other filling up that compost container. In go the soggy teabags and coffee grounds, the leftover salad, wilted flowers from a vase.

Once, she won hands down when she composted our Christmas wreath by nipping it into tiny pieces with her garden shears. She's the queen of compost.

Over the years, the contributions to the compost pile took on a distinctively childish note: half-chewed slices of apple, stray grapes that rolled in the dust, gnawed-upon celery sticks.

One night as I watched our daughter's dish of peas growing cold, I actually heard myself say, "There are hungry children in the world who would love to eat that."

As if on cue, she rolled her eyes. "If I eat two peas, do I still get dessert?"

At least the vegetables aren't completely wasted, going back into the soil to grow more. That's the appeal of composting, I think, that nothing ever truly goes to waste.

Ashes to ashes. Dust to dust. Compost to compost.

There's also a certain amount of art to composting. Good compost is not spontaneous but requires turning the pile with a pitchfork and adding water when things are dry. It also requires a catalyst, usually some rabbit or horse manure. Certain ingredi-ents, such as grass clippings and autumn leaves, must be used sparingly lest they sour the mix.

Composting also follows the seasons. The springtime sun brings a burst of activity to the compost pile. The ingredients are mixed and quickly turn to thick, black loam. Summer's grass clippings, bolted lettuce, beet greens, and damaged vegetables create a heap that threatens to topple over. But heat, rain, and a healthy dose of catalyst quickly bring on a healthy state of rot.

By fall, you can spend a Saturday afternoon spreading some of that compost and cleaning out the pile. Winter is down time to absorb last Halloween's jack-o-lanterns and the occasional wilted poinsettia.

When spring comes round, it's time to do it all over again.

Proper tending of a compost pile brings rewards that go far beyond gardening. After all, we can all use more time just to think, and there's nothing better for letting the thoughts wander than taking pitchfork in hand and mixing that compost heap.

There's an old platitude about the things in life that don't destroy us only making us stronger, but I'm not so sure I believe that. Sometimes I think life wears us down like the wind and rain scouring the sides of an old barn, or maybe the way a thou-sand footsteps polish stone.

If anything, the challenges of life are more like composting—a bit of sadness here, a disappointment there mixed in with all the remnants of good things—leaving us a richness in which our selves take deeper root and grow.

Just as with our backyard garden we can't always predict exactly what part of us will flourish and what will not, but we should always remember that the compost of our experiences is not a scrap heap but instead, the stuff of life.

ORIGINALLY PUBLISHED IN *DELMARVA QUARTERLY*, Autumn 2004.

DELMARVESE

As if anyone needed further proof that Delmarva is a place unto itself, the people speak a different tongue. This language of the land between the bays is known as Delmarvese. You've heard it, even if you haven't put a name to it. It's that unique pronunciation that signals you're from here and everybody else isn't.

Caught me some feesh. Gaoin downy oh-shun. Eat some cray-abs.

Delmarva accents (Eastern Shore accents) have twangy vowels, punctuated by a long "o" sound. It's an accent that's distinctly Southern in its own way. My first real introduction to this matter of local pronunciation occurred when I moved to Cecil County. I pronounced it *See-cil*. But old-timers insist on *Sissal* or even *Sessal*—much as the first English settlers would have said it.

Linguists will tell you that Delmarva's unique way of speaking goes beyond mere accent. Delmarvese is a recognized dialect—a unique pattern of speech—that has its roots in the Elizabethan adventurers who arrived in Shakespeare's era.

One of the ways dialect survives is through isolation, which is why it lasted so long on Delmarva.

"That is one of the factors. But it's not that people don't have access to other dialects through television and other media," explained Tonia Bleam, lecturer in the Department of Linguistics at the University of Maryland. "There's also a sense of identity. Speaking in a dialect might not be that conscious of a thing. But if you start to talk differently, your friends might think you are putting on airs. You might have different ways of speaking in different situations, such as when dealing with outsiders."

Isolation certainly plays a role in places such as Smith Island and Tangier Island. These remote islands in Chesapeake Bay are recognized as having some of the truest Elizabethan dialects. But what does that mean?

Experts say centuries ago, the English language reached a fork in the road. Modern British—the kind we hear on BBC shows today—stayed at home but followed a path of change and evolution. The English spoken by the Elizabethan explorers, soldiers and settlers who came to early America, stayed right here and did not evolve as much.

Some linguists and Shakespearean scholars make a case that Elizabethan sounded a lot like a Scottish brogue. The verbal tics are easy to pick up on if you know what to listen for.

Vowels like "a" are short and drawn out a little (think *haaave* and *haaat*). The "u" comes out shortened and combined with an *oo* sound (*bush* becomes *boosh*, for example). The biggest difference can be heard in the diphthongs, or vowels placed side by side. Modern English blends the sounds together, but Elizabethans would have pronounced each vowel—why else would they be in the word, right? An Elizabethan would have pronounced *house* as having two syllables ... *huh-oose*. If you listen closely, it all starts to sound rather Delmarvesque.

Beyond accent, sentence structure bears similarities to an older English. A *New York Times* writer described it this way: "Mainlanders say, logically enough, 'Look how blue the sky is.' Not the Shoreman. He says, 'Look at the sky, how blue it is.' " Now that sounds like Shakespeare.

"When we talk about different dialects we are really looking at all levels of structure," Bleam said. While the older forms of English (such as those heard on Delmarva) stay the same, "It's often the standard English that's quickly changing."

You don't have to visit the remote areas of Delmarva to hear this dialect. If you troll YouTube, you will come across videos of locals conversing in their very own lingo.

I experienced this odd phenomenon myself back in 1990, during a visit to the town of Church Creek in Dorchester County. Vast salt marshes surround the town and as you drive into Church Creek you will pass a huge sculpture of a mosquito, which says volumes about this community's sense of humor.

I drove down to Church Creek with a friend who was originally from Harford County in central Maryland, but had taken up residence long enough to join the volunteer fire company and get to know some people in the community. He had since moved away, but took me along for a return visit to Dorchester County. We stopped by the firehouse and talked with a couple of guys he knew. Normal enough. Then a third guy stopped by, and the three of them seemed to forget we were there and started speaking among themselves in a seemingly foreign dialect.

It was spooky, like getting caught up in a time warp. I'd heard about this legendary Elizabethan dialect, but I'd been skeptical. Now I was a believer.

Sadly, it's likely that the unique Delmarva dialect is in danger of dying out. But for now, it always seems like there is still an old-timer somewhere who talks the talk. Last summer, we ran into one selling produce at a roadside stand: "You can go right home now and put that ear in the *booling wooter!*"

Taking the sack filled with ripe sweet corn, it became clear that some Delmarvese requires no translation.

ORIGINALLY PUBLISHED IN *DELMARVA QUARTERLY*, Summer 2009.

GLASS BEACH

In our small town of Chesapeake City, when we took walks with the kids, our destination was often a strip of sand along the Chesapeake and Delaware Canal. This spot doesn't actually have a name; our kids just called it "the beach," but a better name for it might be "Glass Beach" because the sand is littered with broken glass.

No one really knows who owns Glass Beach. Some claim it's property of the U.S. Army Corps of Engineers, which maintains the busy shipping canal. Others say the beach is owned by a nearby restaurant, or maybe the bed and breakfast next door.

It may be that this sense of limbo is why the location has become a de facto public beach, a sandy oasis in what used to be a working waterfront town. There is a pleasant air of neglect about this spot. A sagging dock runs parallel to shore, one side propped up with a stack of concrete blocks. A sign warns against swimming. This is a beach for looking and playing, not wading. The steep drop of the canal and swift currents make venturing into the water too dangerous.

At high tide, water sloshes under the dock, reaching out to further erode the shore. Not more than 30 feet long, the beach stops at a jumble of rocks at one end. On the other side, a stand of mulberry trees is slowly being pried loose from its grip on the land, orange roots clutching at air. Every year another tree falls victim to the tide and is swept off in a nor'easter. The trees that remain hang over the water's edge, looking forlorn, awaiting their doom.

The beach has been the scene of small adventures and drama. Once, we watched a man with a dog throw a stick too far out into the canal. His dog swam out and was caught in the current.

"Swim, Kane, swim!" he cried, seeing the dog spin like a scrap of flotsam. Stick in mouth, the dog struggled, started to go under. "Kane!" the man called shrilly. Then all at once the current let go like a hand releasing its grip. The dog reached shore and shook itself. The man took the stick and held it like it was something dangerous, a betrayal. When the dog wasn't looking he tossed it away.

Winter at the beach has its own charms and dangers. When there is a good hard freeze, ice rafts far out into the canal, into the shipping channel. The ice is deceptively inviting, a pristine arctic pathway, but the shifting currents rot it from beneath. Only a fool would try to cross this ice.

Once, years before we had our own kids, my wife and I were out walking on a crystalline January day. We were passing the beach when we spotted children on the ice, three small figures adventuring across the floes above where the channel drops off. We could see the danger they were in, though the children could not. My wife's voice surrounded them like a thrown rope: "Get off that ice right now!" The oldest one, no more than eight, cast surly glances our way as the trio slipped and slid ashore, then walked away through town. "I didn't want to see anyone die today," said my wife, shivering.

The beach can be a gentle place as well. It's a good spot for holding hands. Late at night, couples have been known to sneak away to that sandy cove. Sometimes in the confusion of darkness they leave behind their blankets and stray flip-flops, the wrack line of love.

When we had children of our own, the little beach became a destination for evening walks, a place to skip stones and gather polished beach glass.

The source of the glass on the beach is a matter of speculation. Most likely, it came from a nearby tavern that has stood near that spot since the early 1800s. The tavern has undergone various incarnations. Canal diggers drank here in the early days, then biker gangs in the 1960s and '70s, and now well-heeled visitors to the gourmet restaurant on the canalfront hoist their glasses.

Long-ago revelers must have spilled out from the tavern and shattered their bottles on the rocks, leaving the broken glass to glimmer at night like stars, the bits too numerous to count or ever clean up.

Some of the oldest pieces have been polished into beach glass by the tumbling action of waves and sand. Every now and then we find old bits of pottery, broken plates and stoneware bottles, their glazed surfaces crackled by time. We filled old Mason jars with the beach glass and gave them away to friends, although we kept one jar that now sits on a bookshelf. Not all the glass is smooth; going barefoot on the beach is inviting an accident, like dancing in a rose garden.

But the glass does give the beach a certain character. When the wake from passing boats rolls in at low tide it catches the glass and rolls it among the pebbles, so that the waves tinkle and shimmer. It's a sound like wind chimes. Wave chimes, you might say.

Besides the glass and bits of broken plates, there are other hints of the past. A set of railroad tracks runs into the water, going nowhere. The ties are waterlogged and slick, the iron rails rusting in the brackish water. A century ago the tracks carried lumber and ripe watermelons onto barges for the trip to Baltimore or Philadelphia.

Times change. The tide goes in; the tide goes out. Somehow, the years have passed and our children are grown. That

Mason jar filled with beach glass is now a dusty jar of memories.

Evening is still the best time at Glass Beach. When the sun goes down the last rays turn the water a lush island blue like a Cezanne painting. Neighbors gather to trade town gossip and watch the boats go by. Kids prod the sand with sticks or throw corn to the ducks. Moms and dads sit on the old dock and watch. "The beach" or "Glass Beach," call it what you will, we know it's a place where something's always going on.

These moments at the beach may be fleeting. Each year, the sagging dock comes closer to washing away. Lately, I have noticed that the entire beach itself is in danger of eroding and disappearing, so walk there soon with your children or your sweetheart, while you can. You may be grateful for that memory someday. The tide is relentless, my friend.

ORIGINALLY PUBLISHED IN *DELMARVA QUARTERLY*, Autumn 2006.

ABOUT THE AUTHOR

David Healey lives in Maryland where he worked as a journalist for more than 20 years. He is a member of the International Thriller Writers and the Eastern Shore Writers Association. Visit him online at www.davidhealeyauthor.com or www. facebook.com/david.healey.books

Thank you for reading! If you enjoyed the book, please consider leaving a review on Amazon.com.

www.ingramcontent.com/pod-product-compliance
Lightning Source LLC
Chambersburg PA
CBHW022146240626
47153CB00007B/2539